PRETTY & TWISTED

Pop Surrealism Adult Coloring Book
Featuring artwork by Heather Rose

I0492996

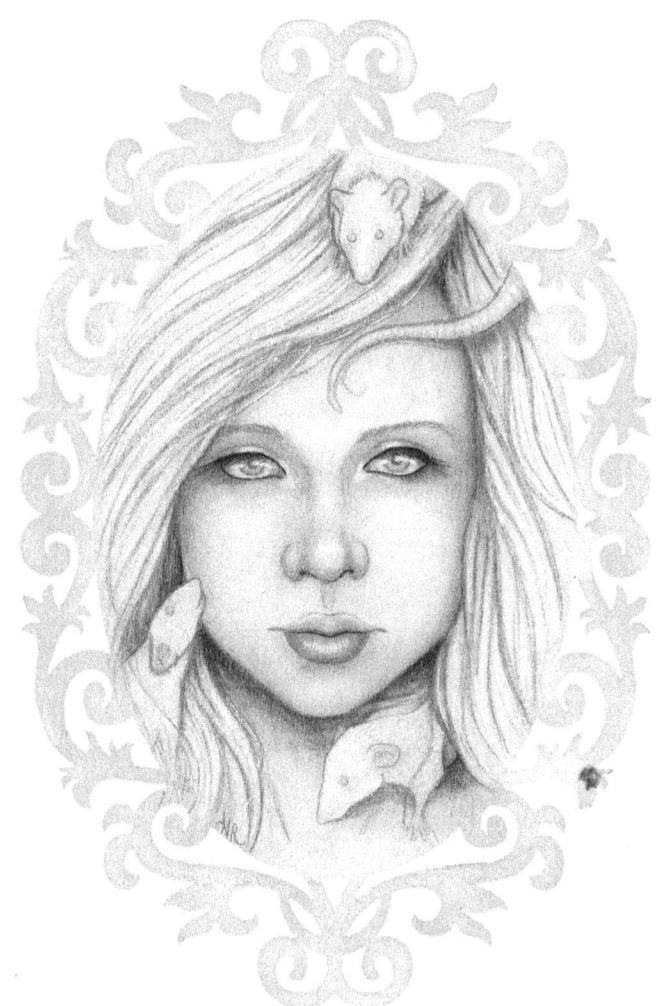

The illustrations in this book are based on original paintings by Heather Rose.
See how the original artworks were colored at
www.HeatherRoseStudios.com

Pretty & Twisted - Pop Surrealism Adult Coloring Book
by Heather Rose
First Published July 2017
ISBN: 978-1533074492

HELPFUL TIPS

Always put a clean sheet of blank paper between the page you are working on and the rest of the pages. It will help prevent markers from bleeding onto the next page!

This book works best with colored pencils and markers. Wet mediums such as paint can soak through the pages.

When using pencils, don't press too hard. Build up color slowly in layers. It's easier to blend and shade this way!

Keep pencils sharp and markers fresh!

Experiment! Just because the original painting was done a certain way doesn't mean you need to color it the same. Have fun with it!

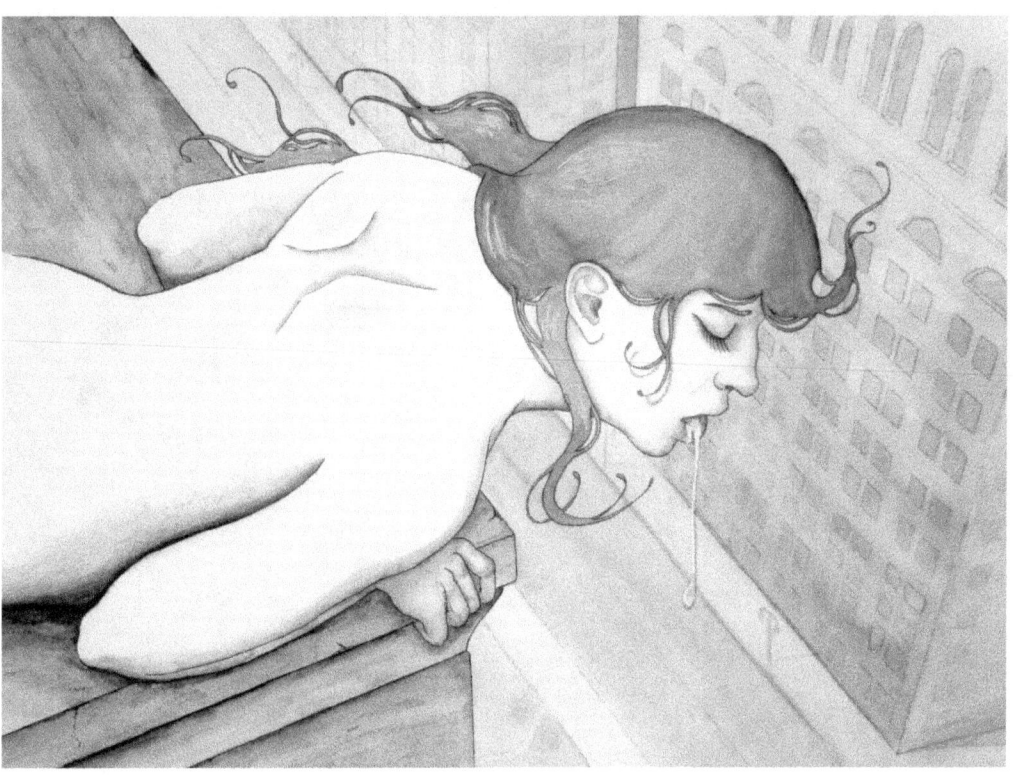

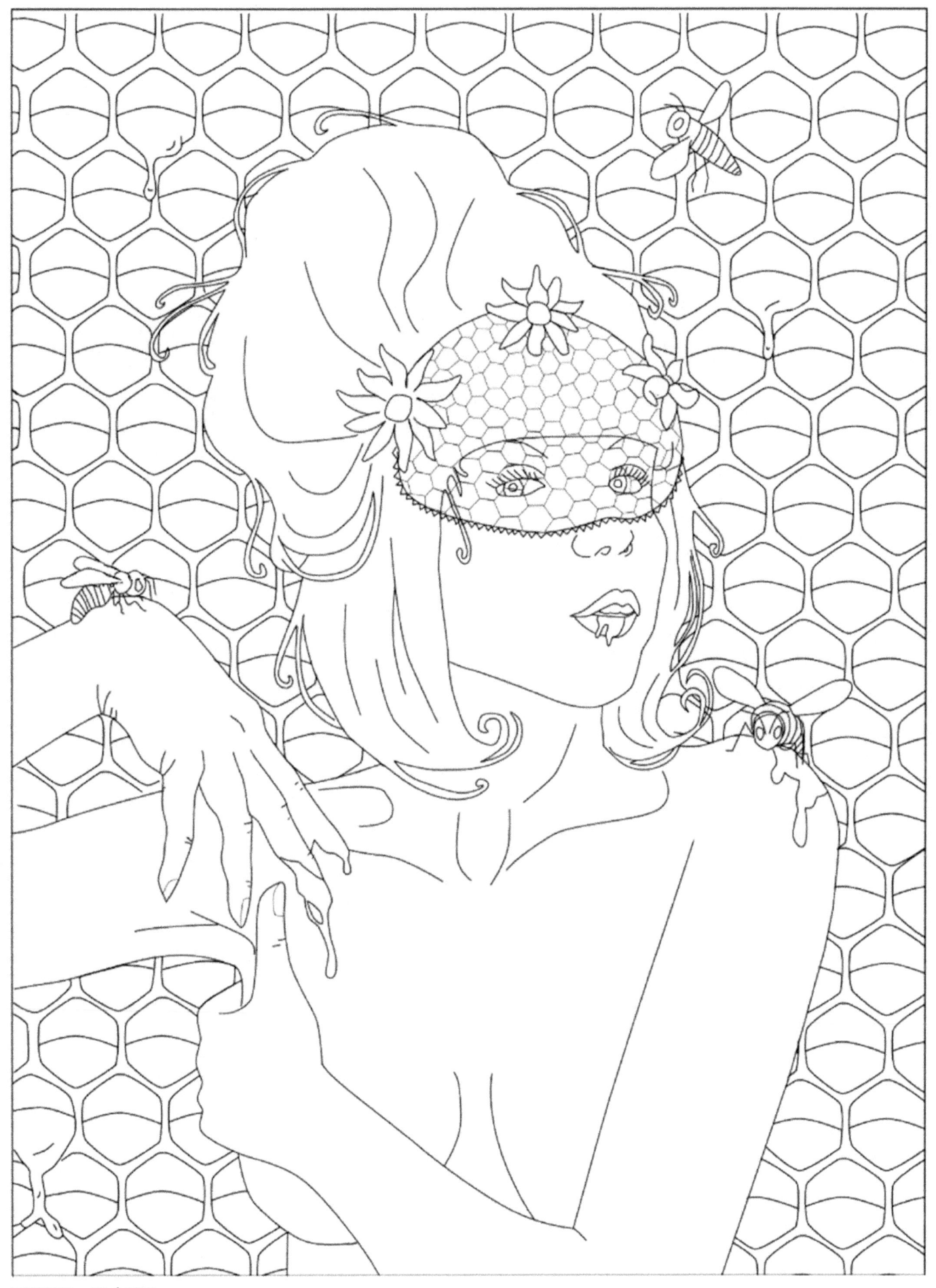

PRETTY & TWISTED

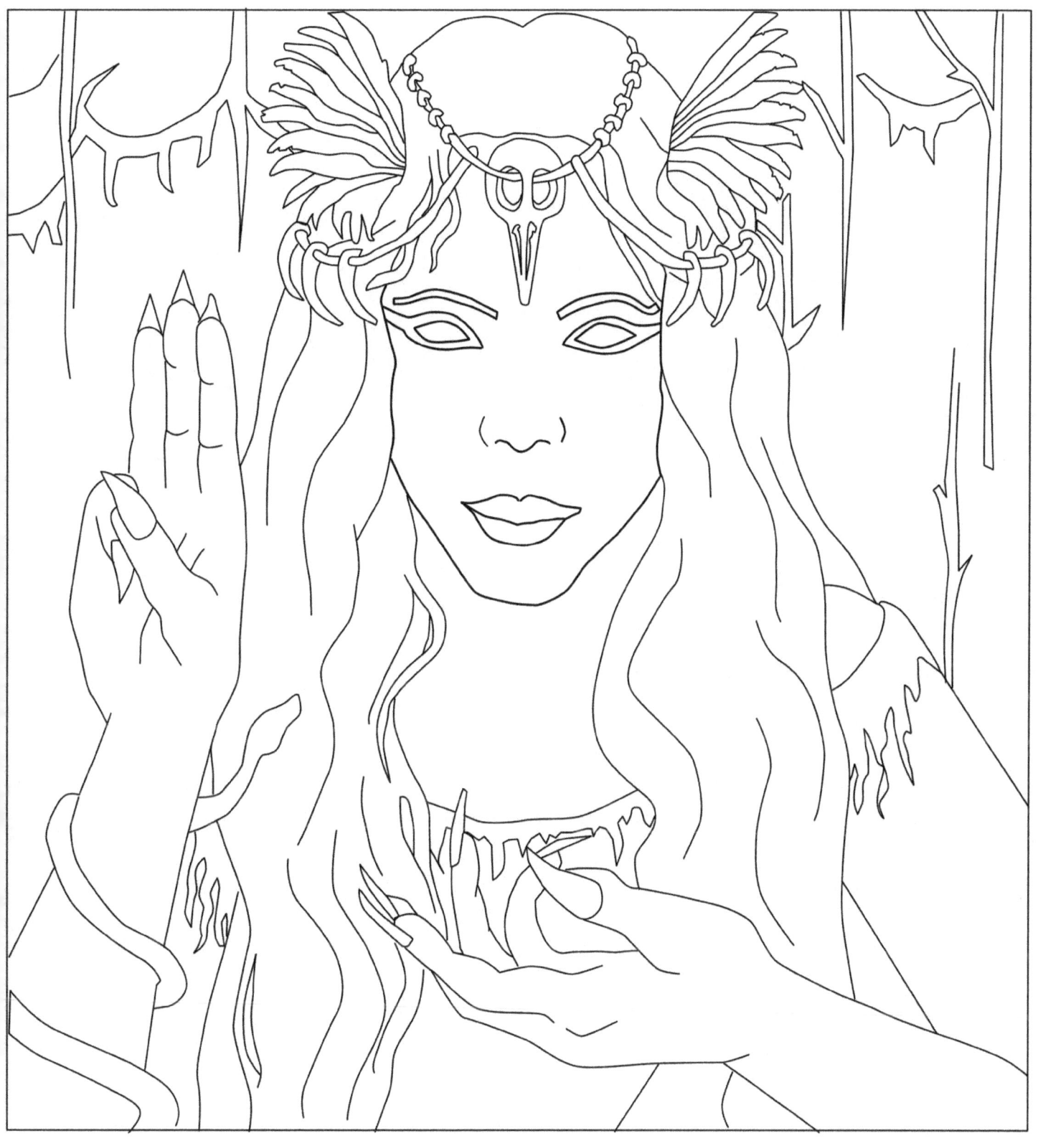

PRETTY & TWISTED

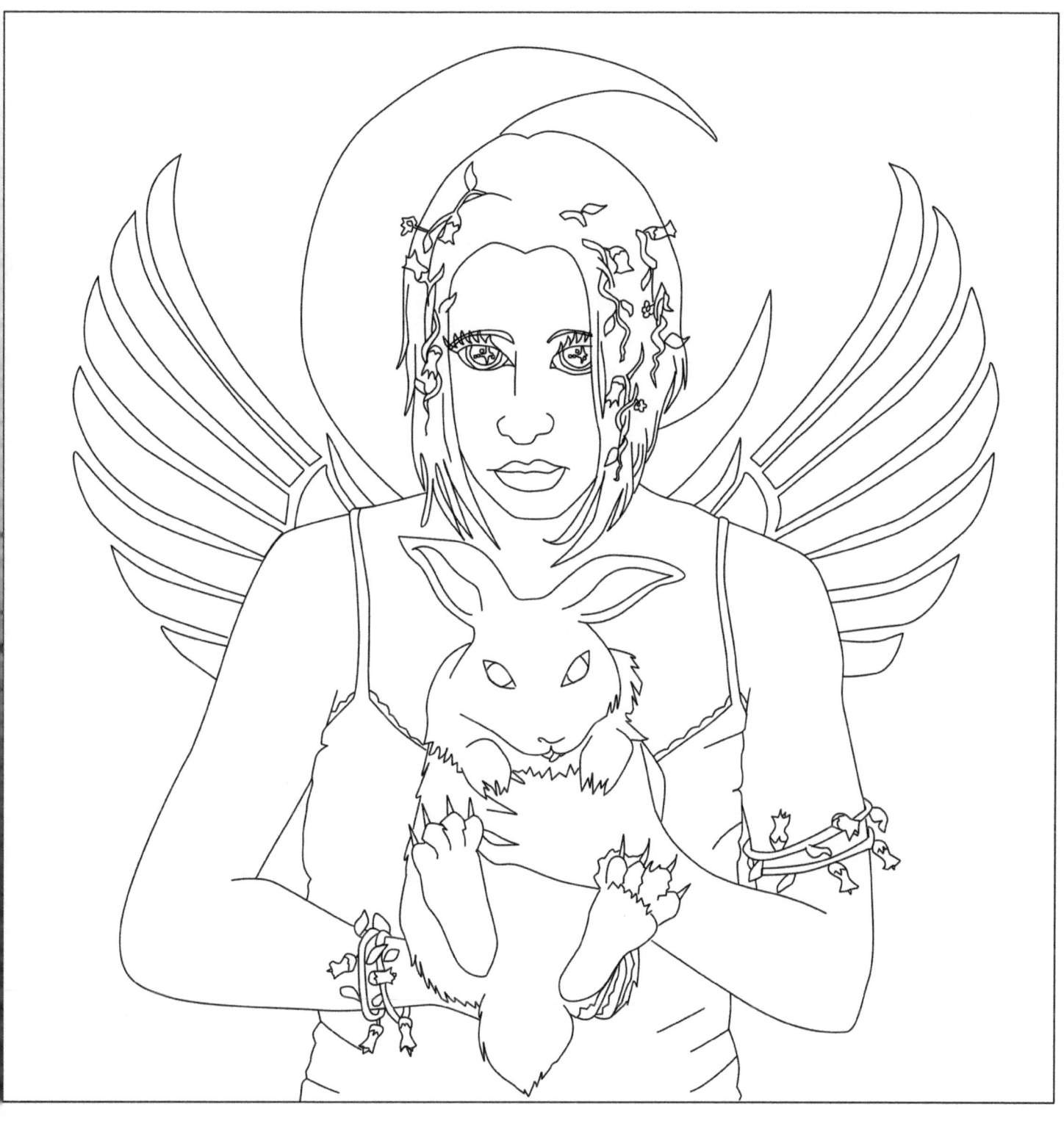

PRETTY & TWISTED

© Heather Rose

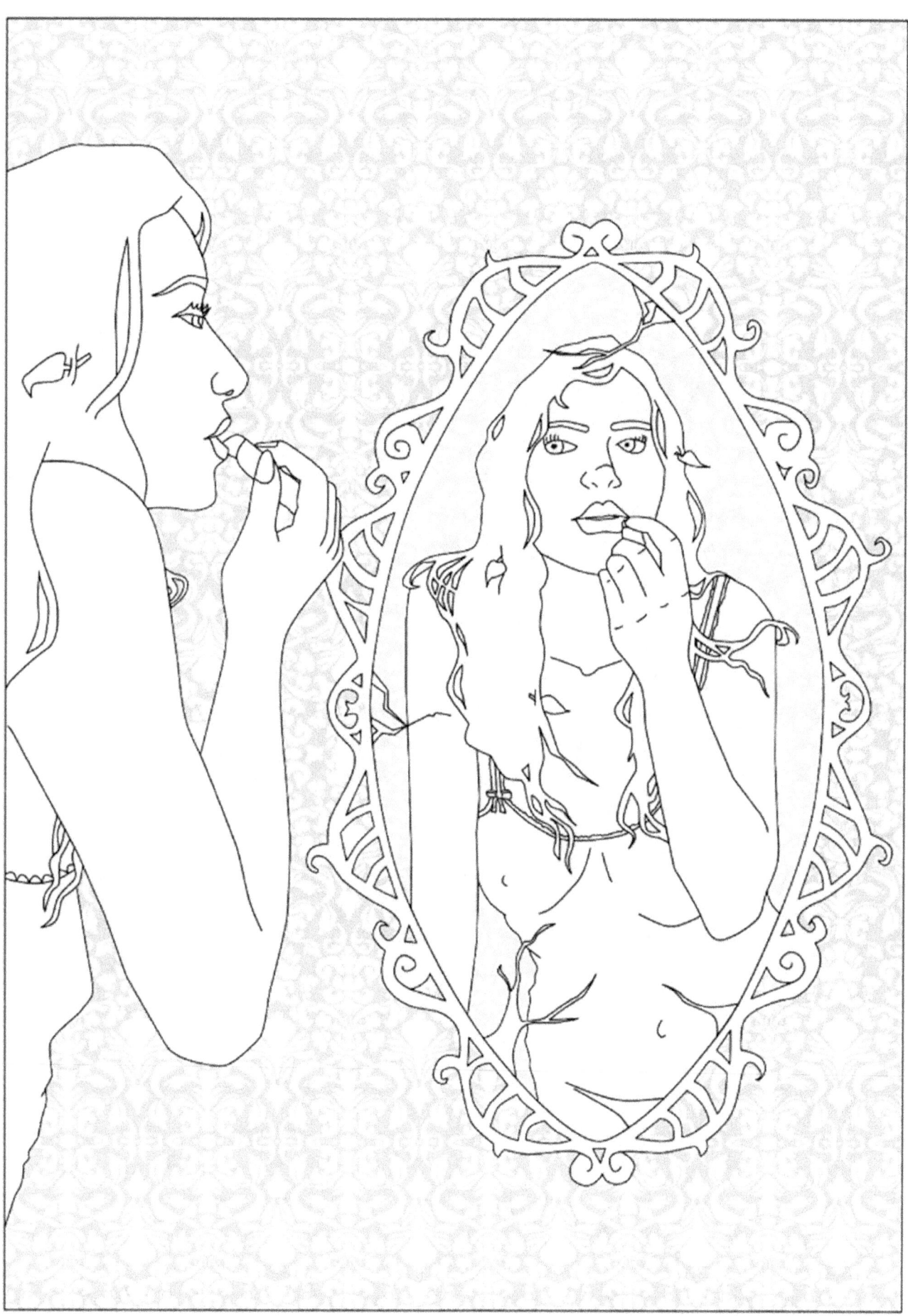

PRETTY & TWISTED

© Heather Rose

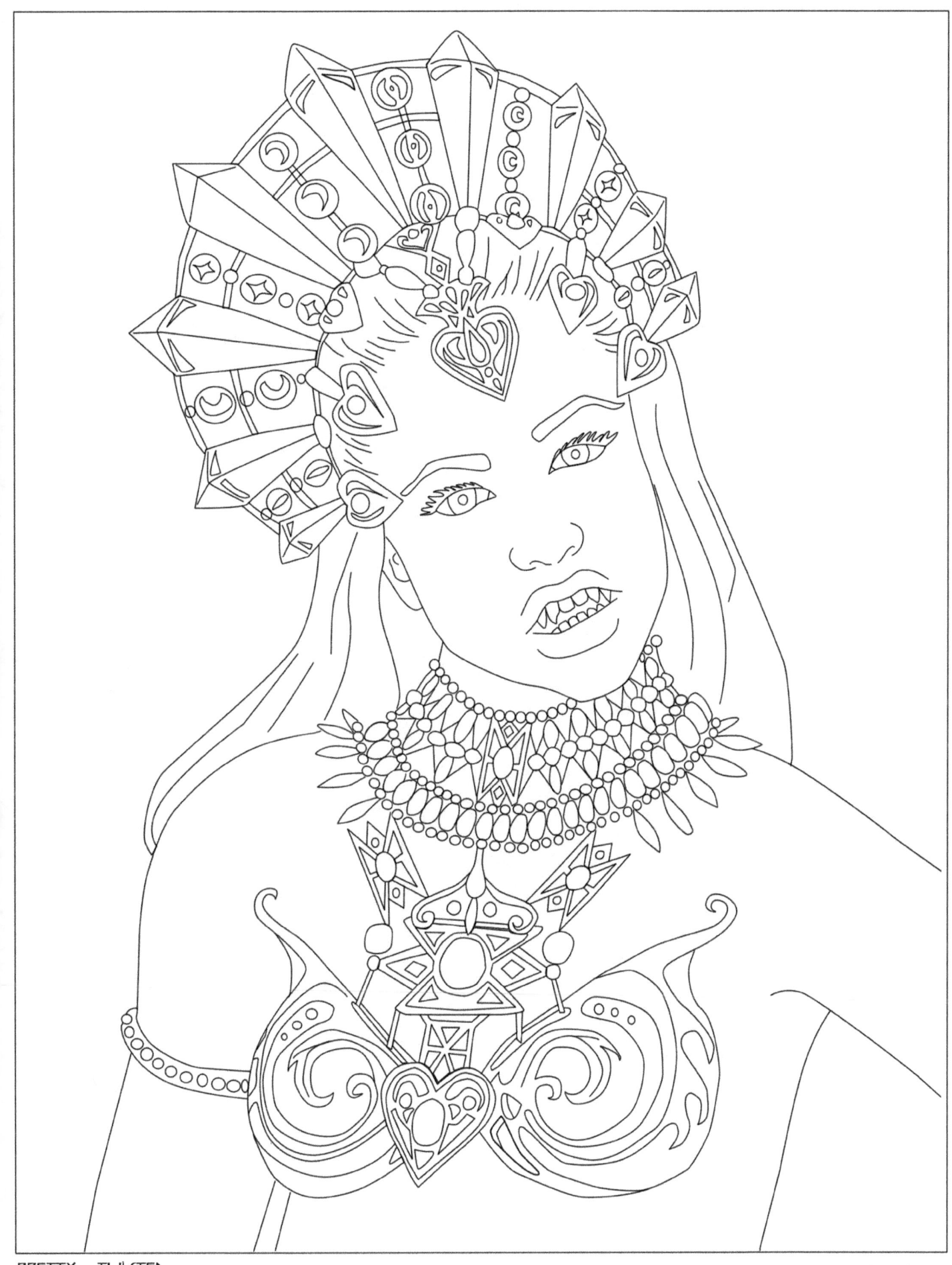

PRETTY & TWISTED

© Heather Rose

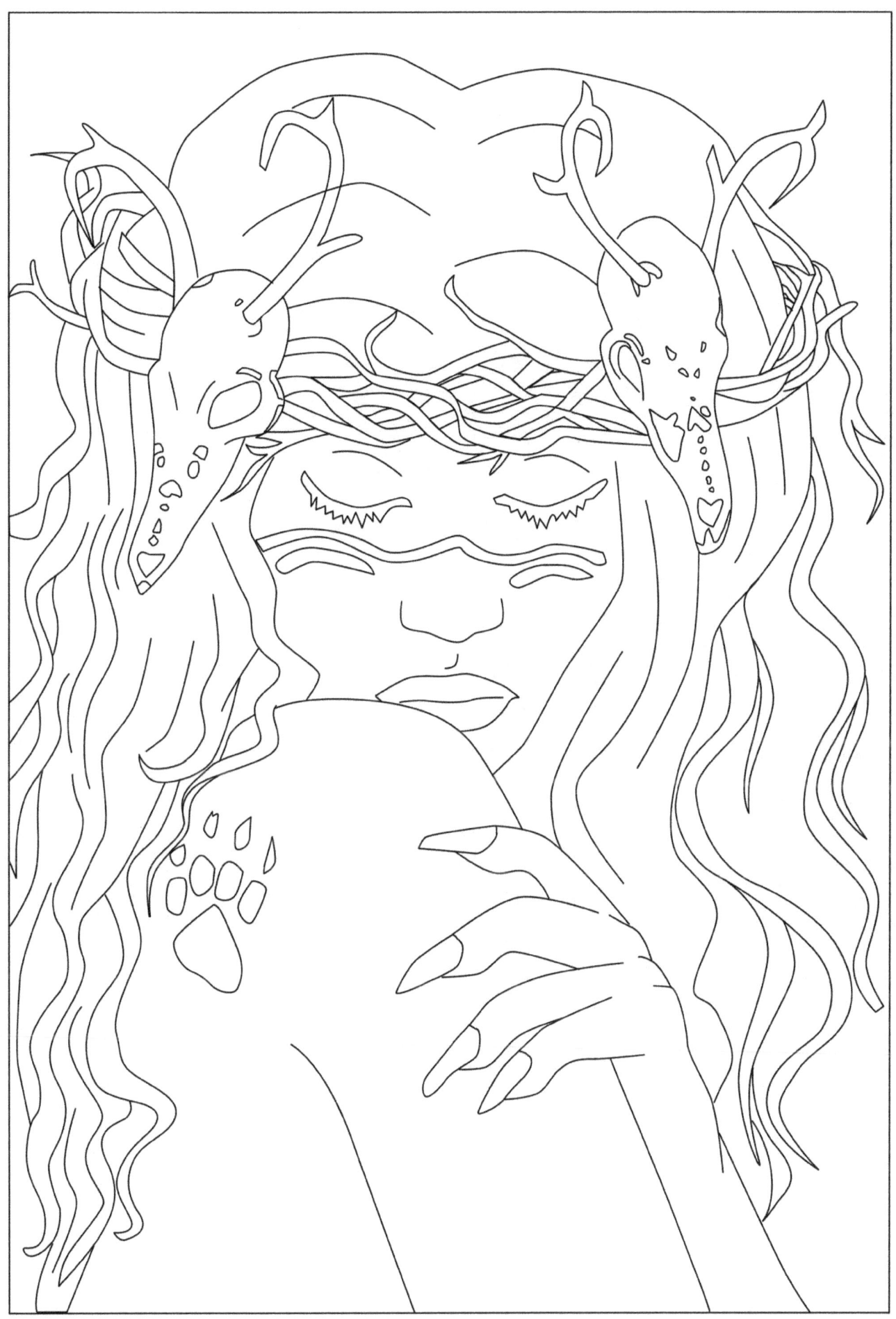

PRETTY & TWISTED   © Heather Rose

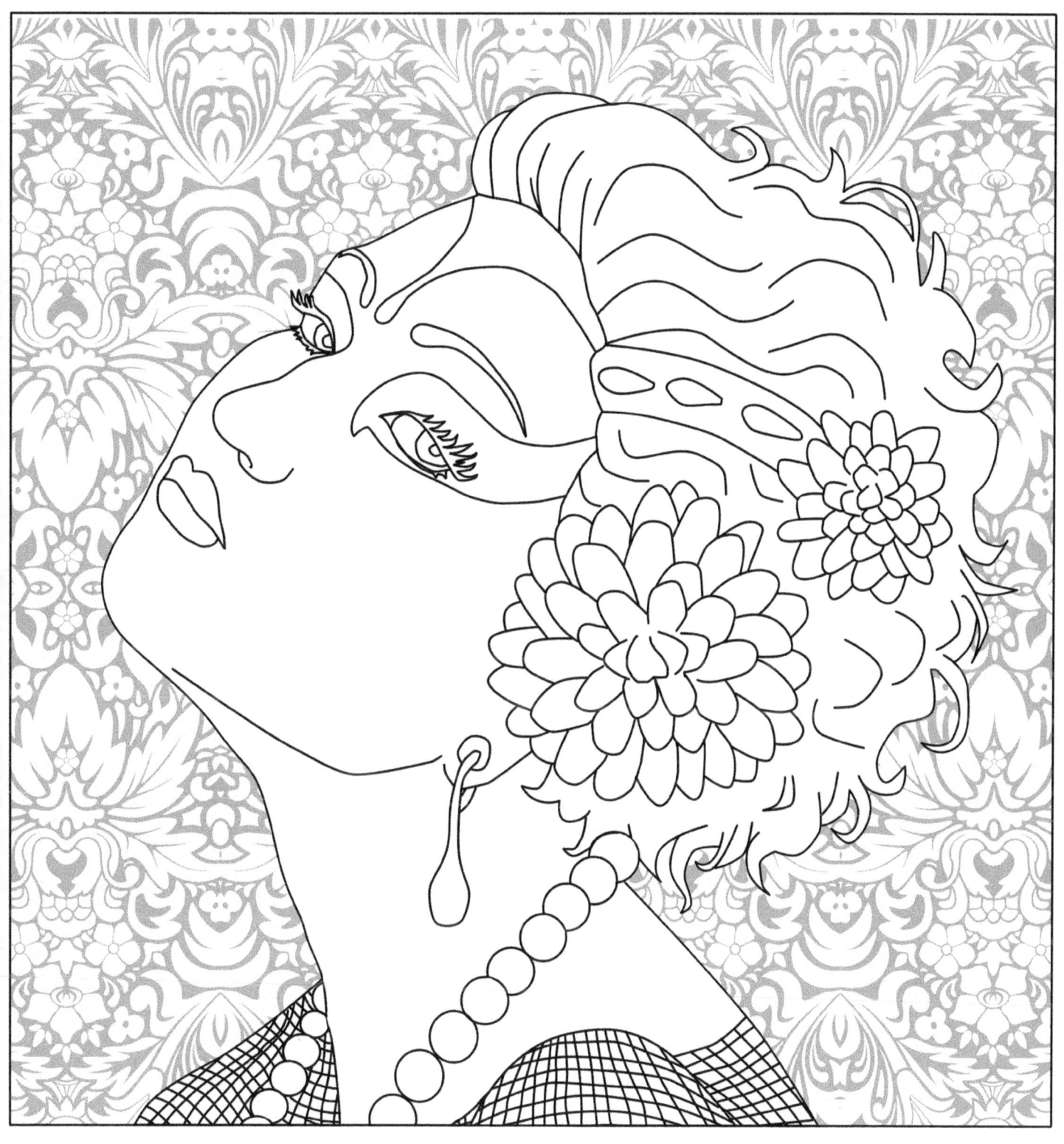

PRETTY & TWISTED

© Heather Rose

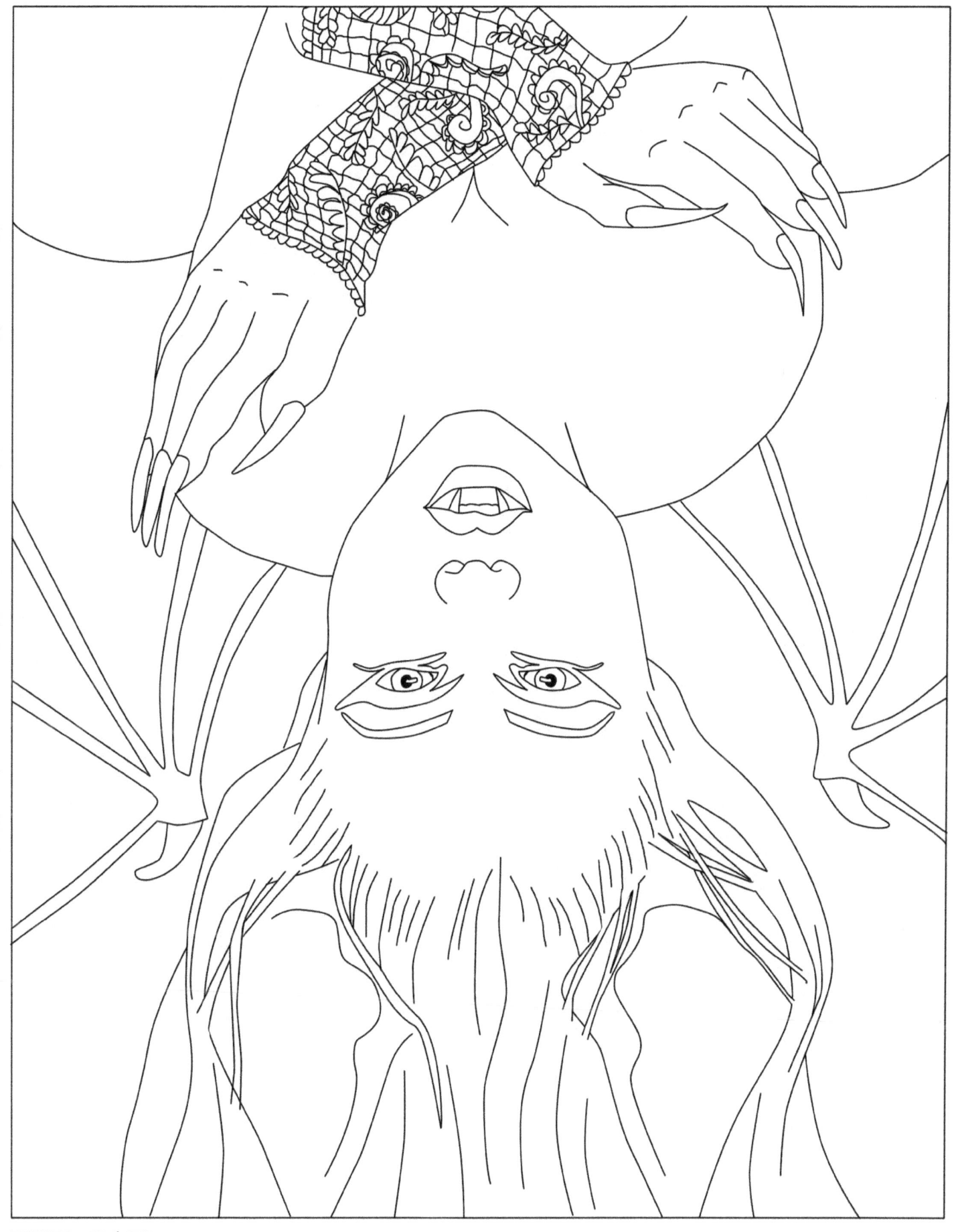

PRETTY & TWISTED

© Heather Rose

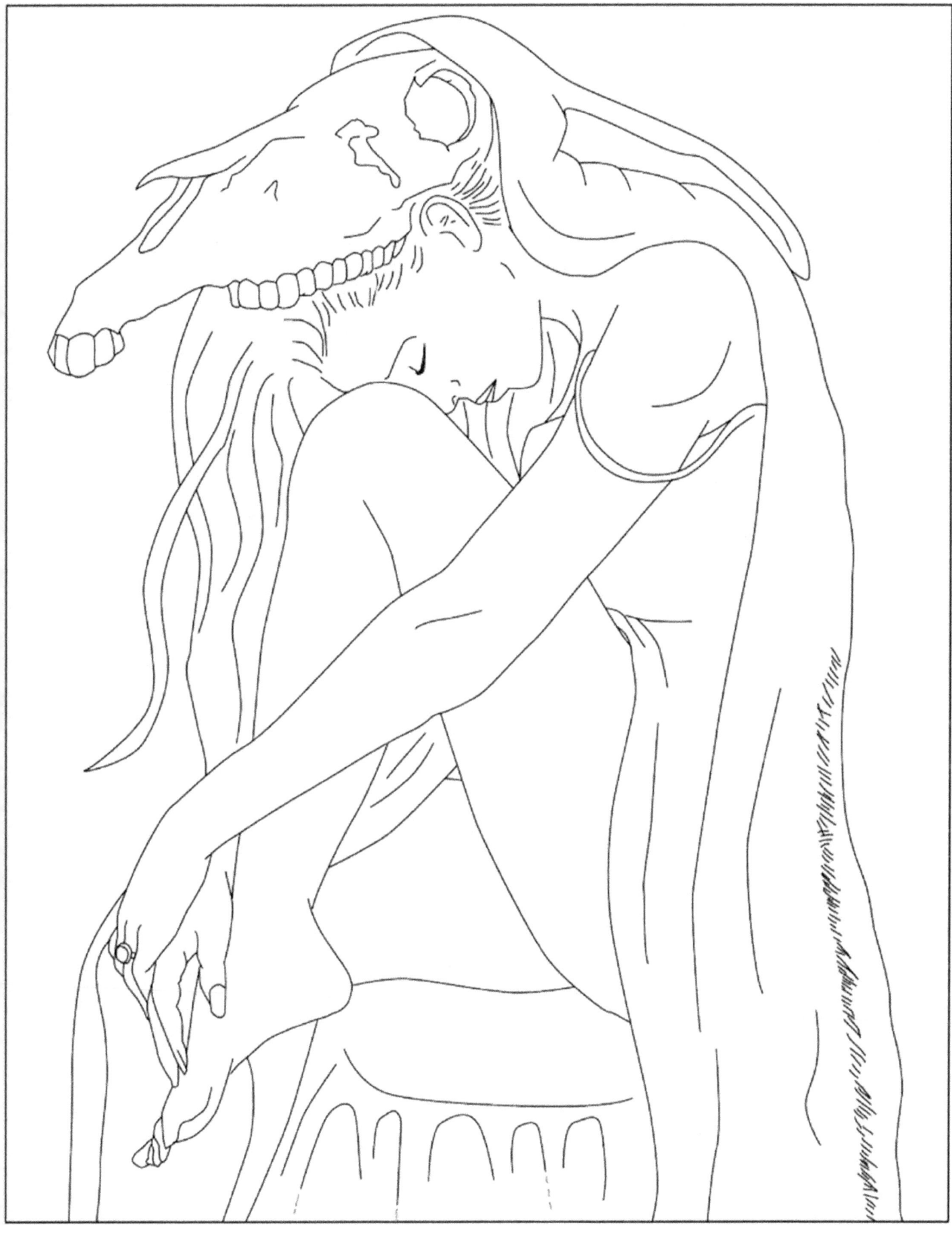

PRETTY & TWISTED

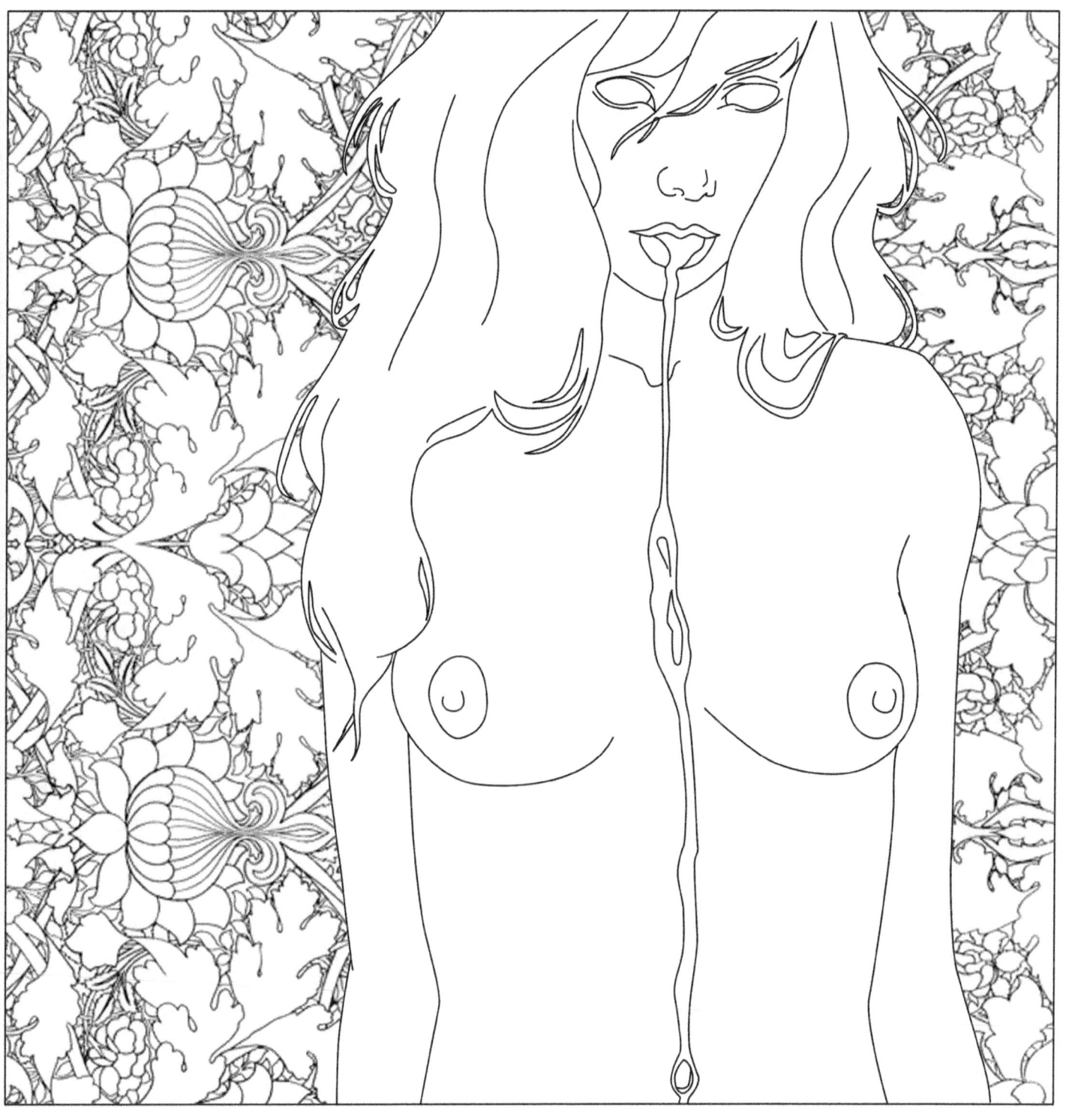

PRETTY & TWISTED

© Heather Rose

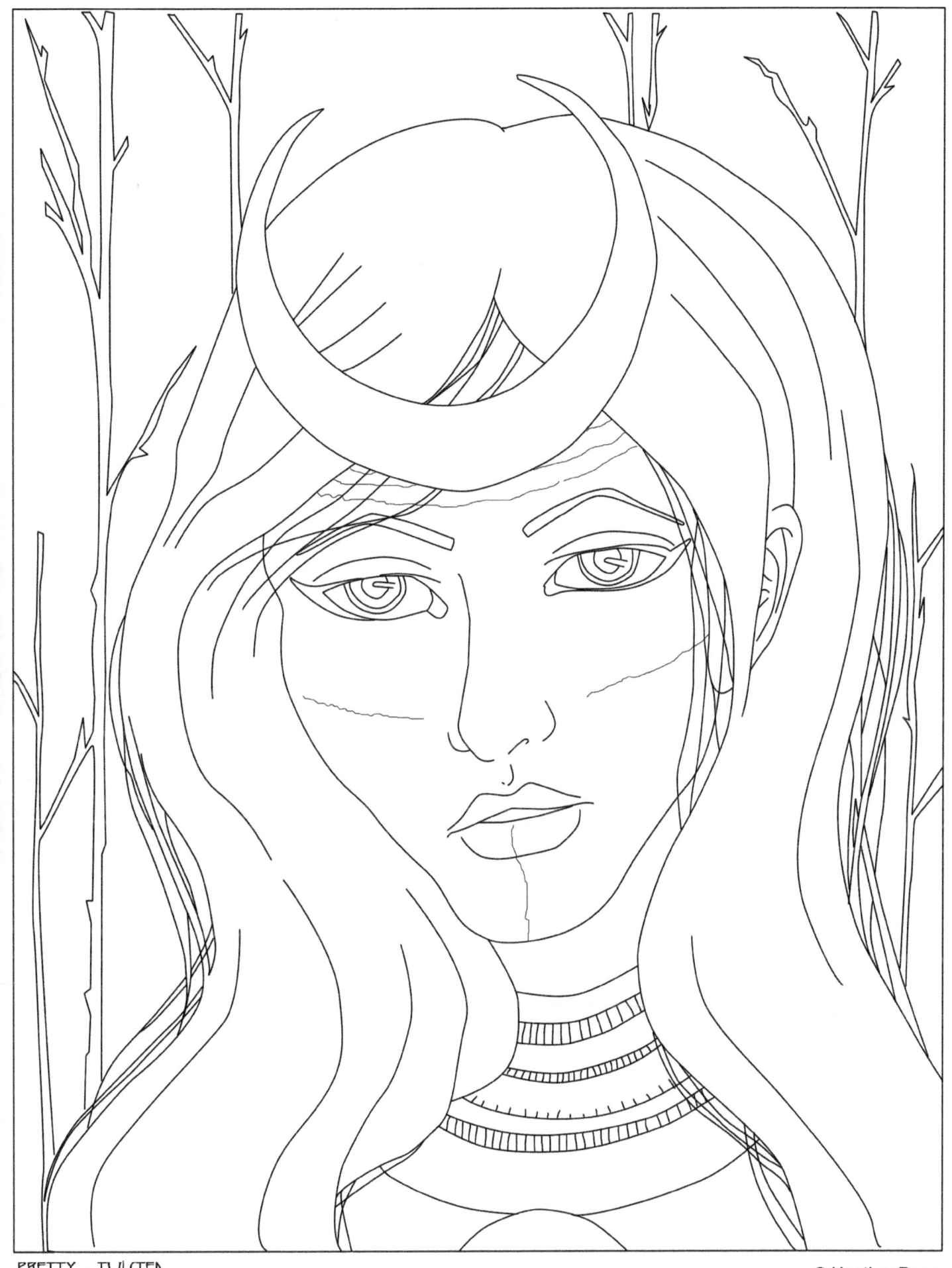

PRETTY & TWISTED

© Heather Rose

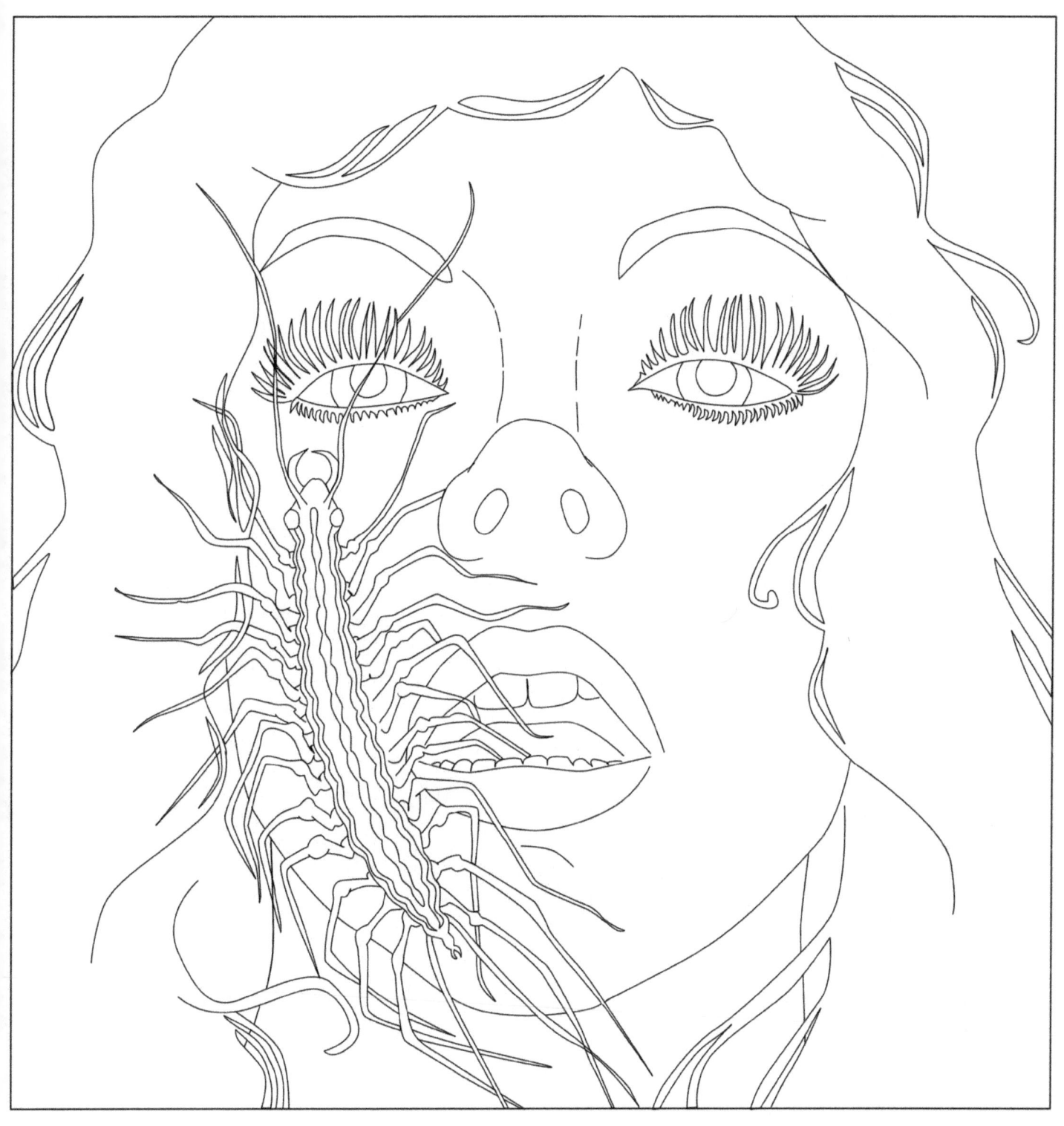

PRETTY & TWISTED

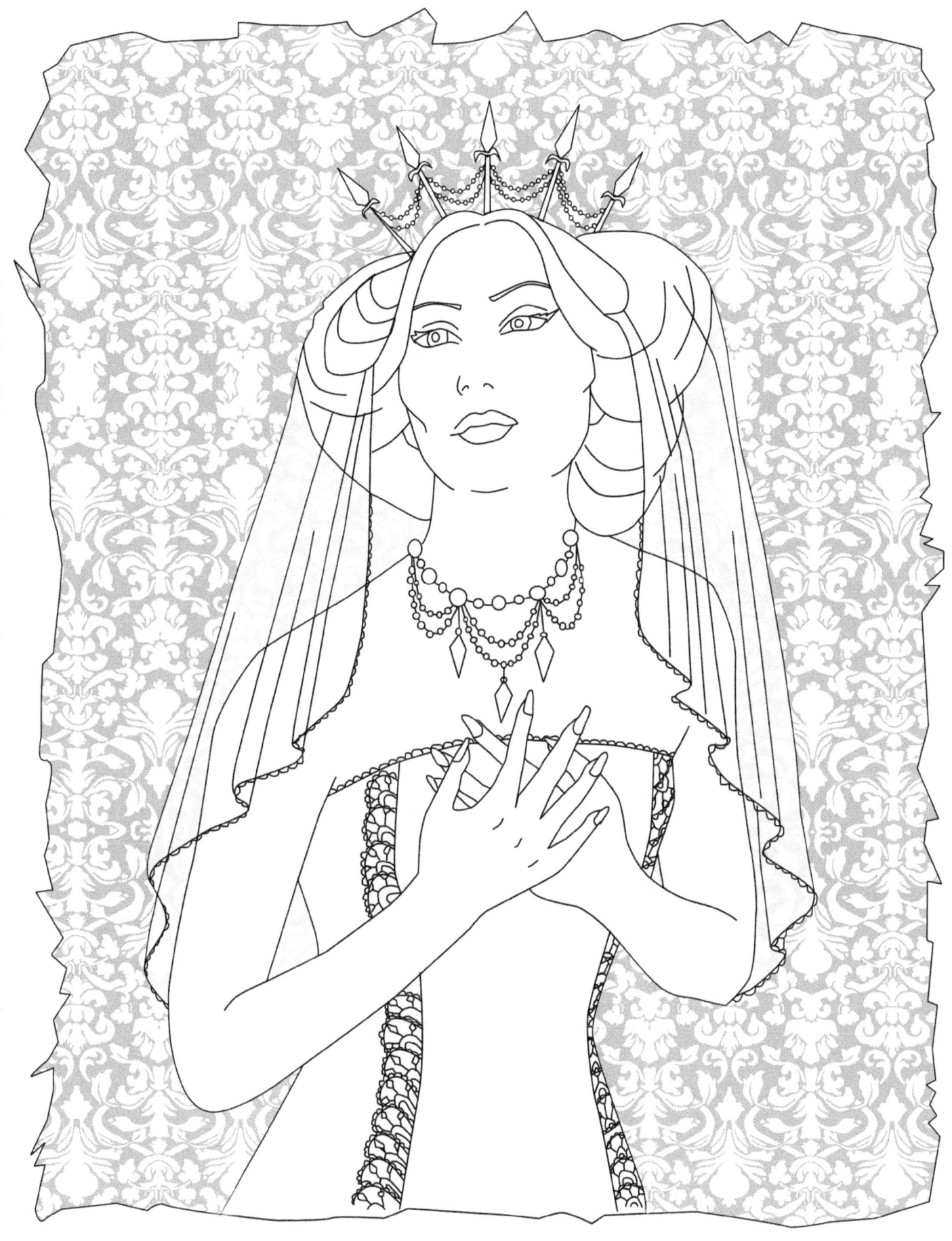

PRETTY & TWISTED

© Heather Rose

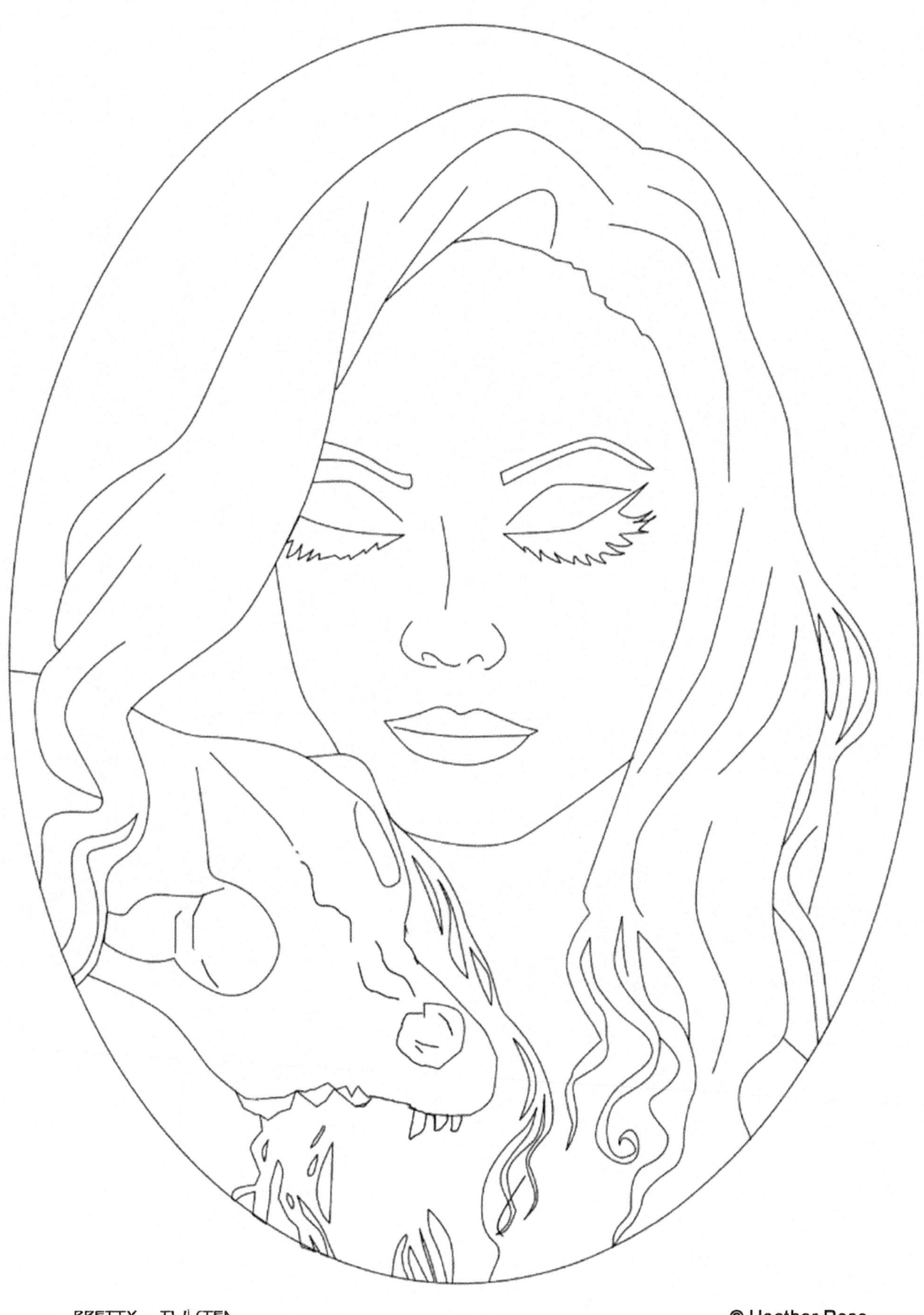

PRETTY & TWISTED

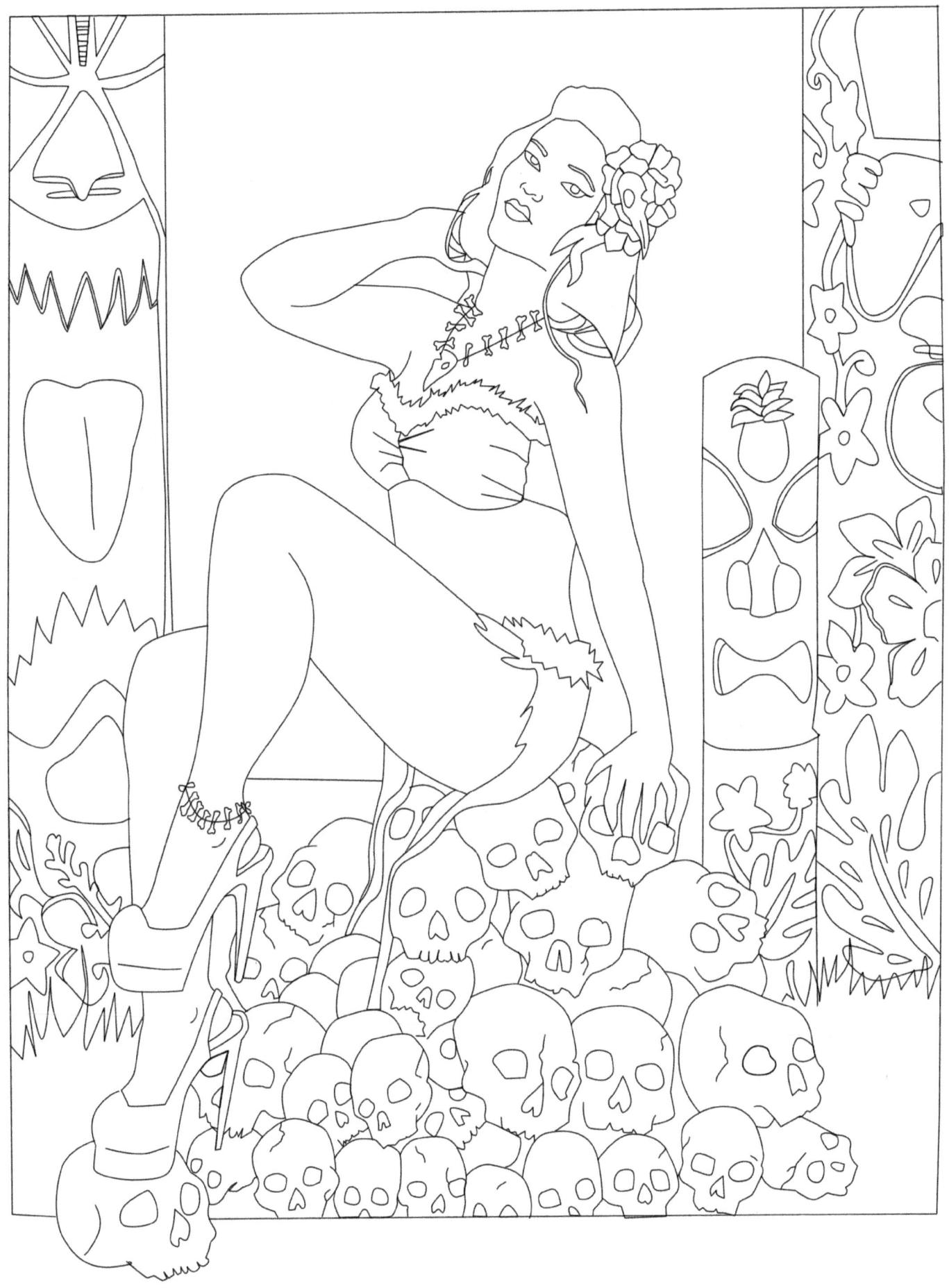

PRETTY & TWISTED

© Heather Rose

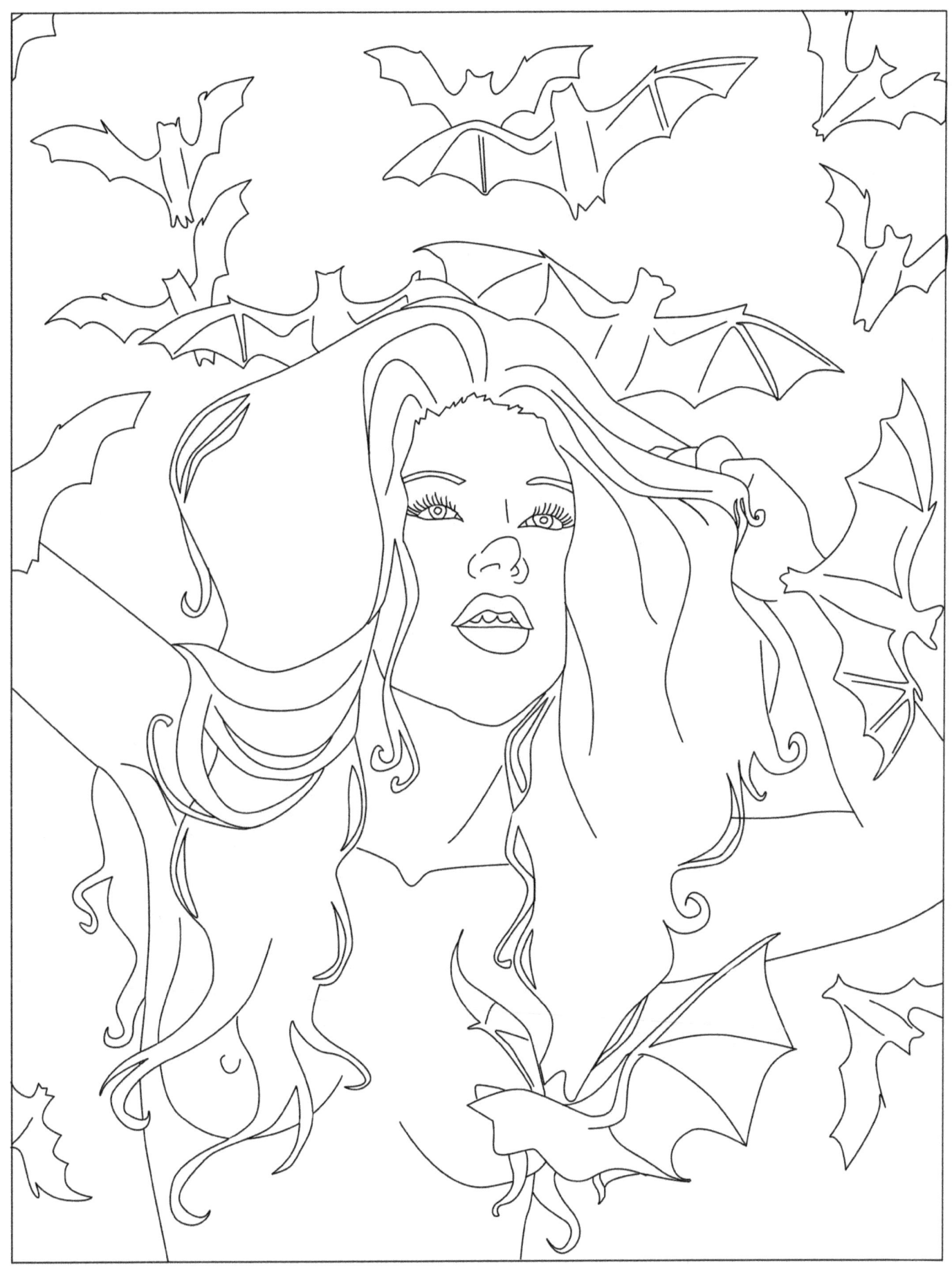

PRETTY & TWISTED

© Heather Rose

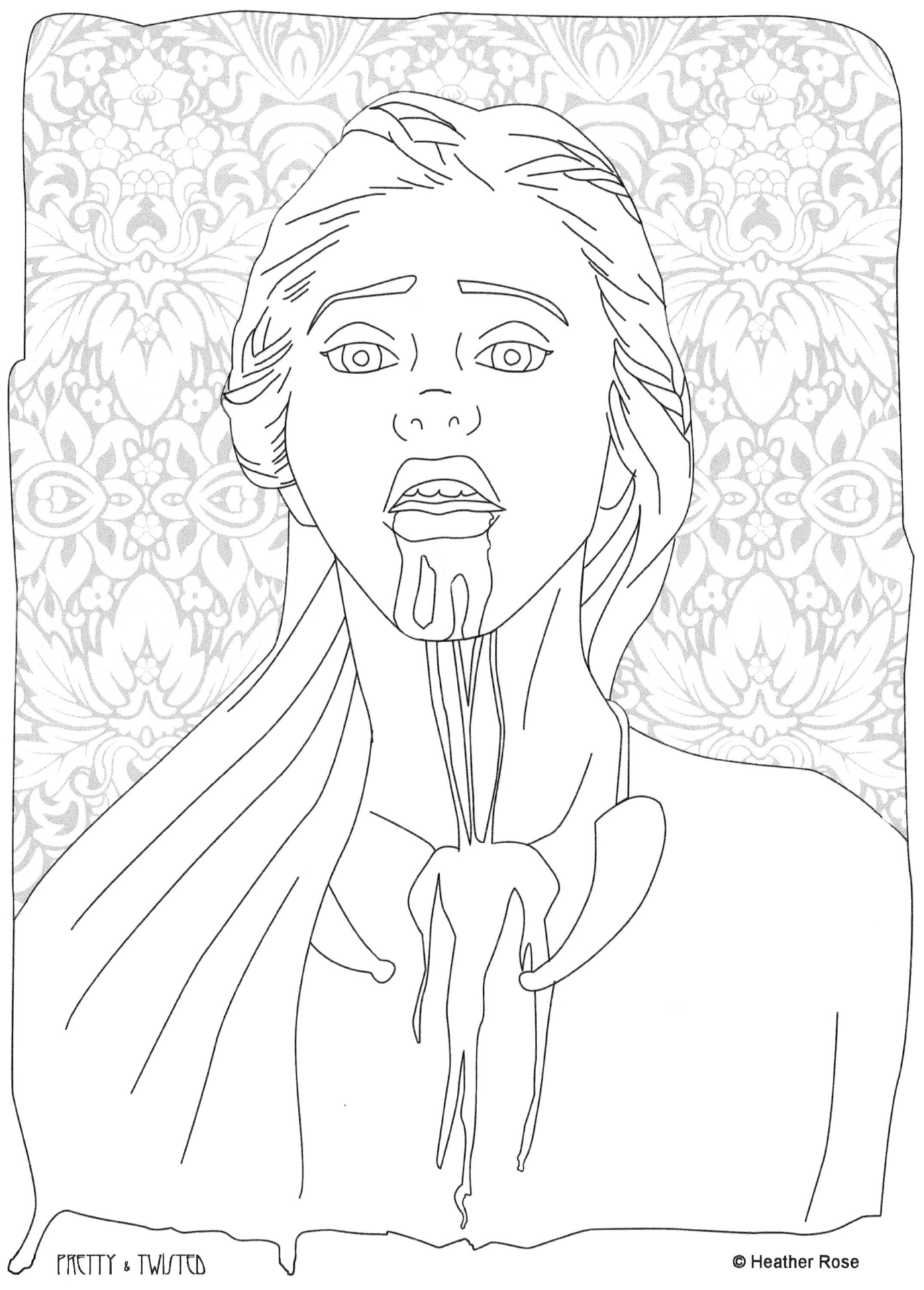

PRETTY & TWISTED

© Heather Rose

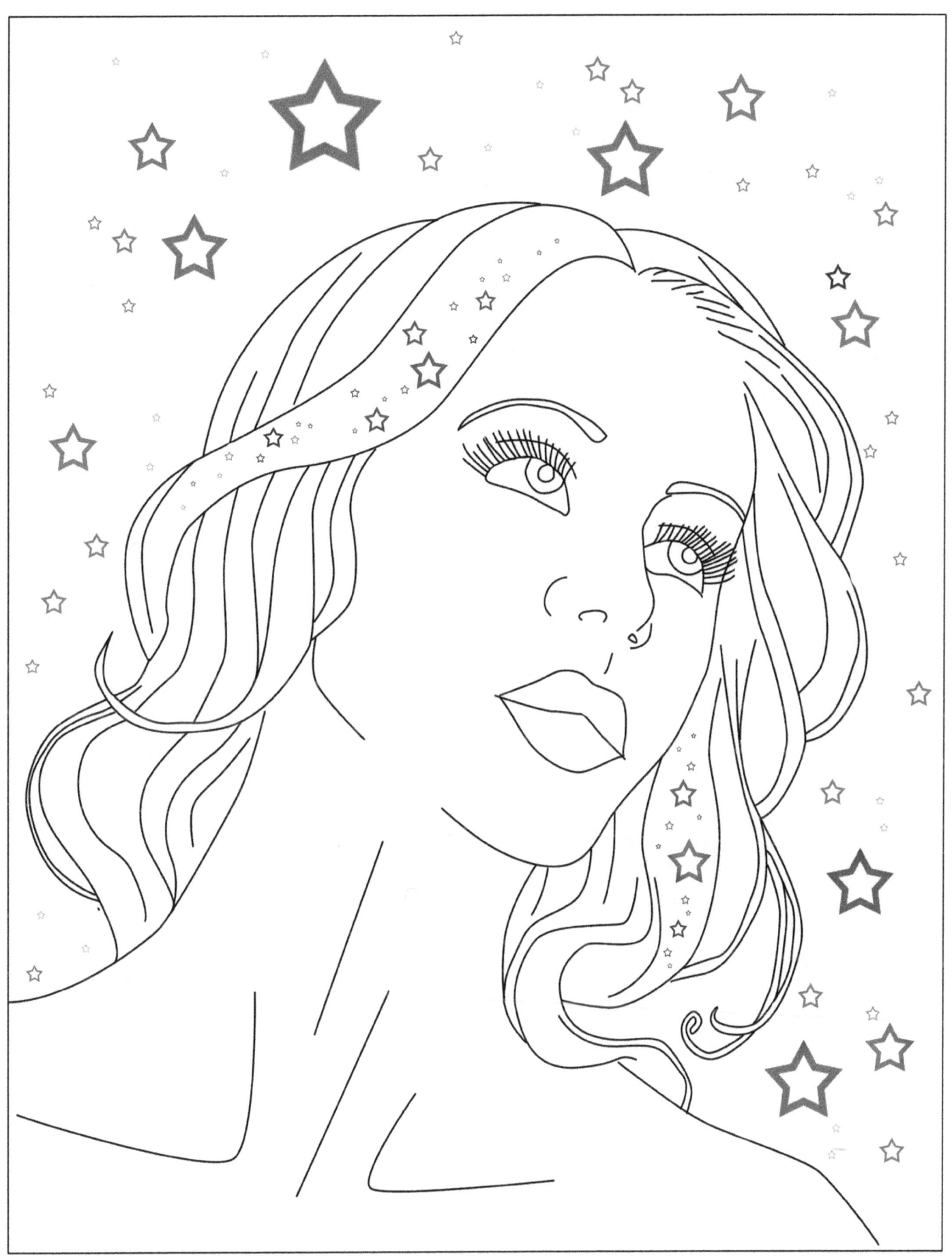

PRETTY & TWISTED

© Heather Rose

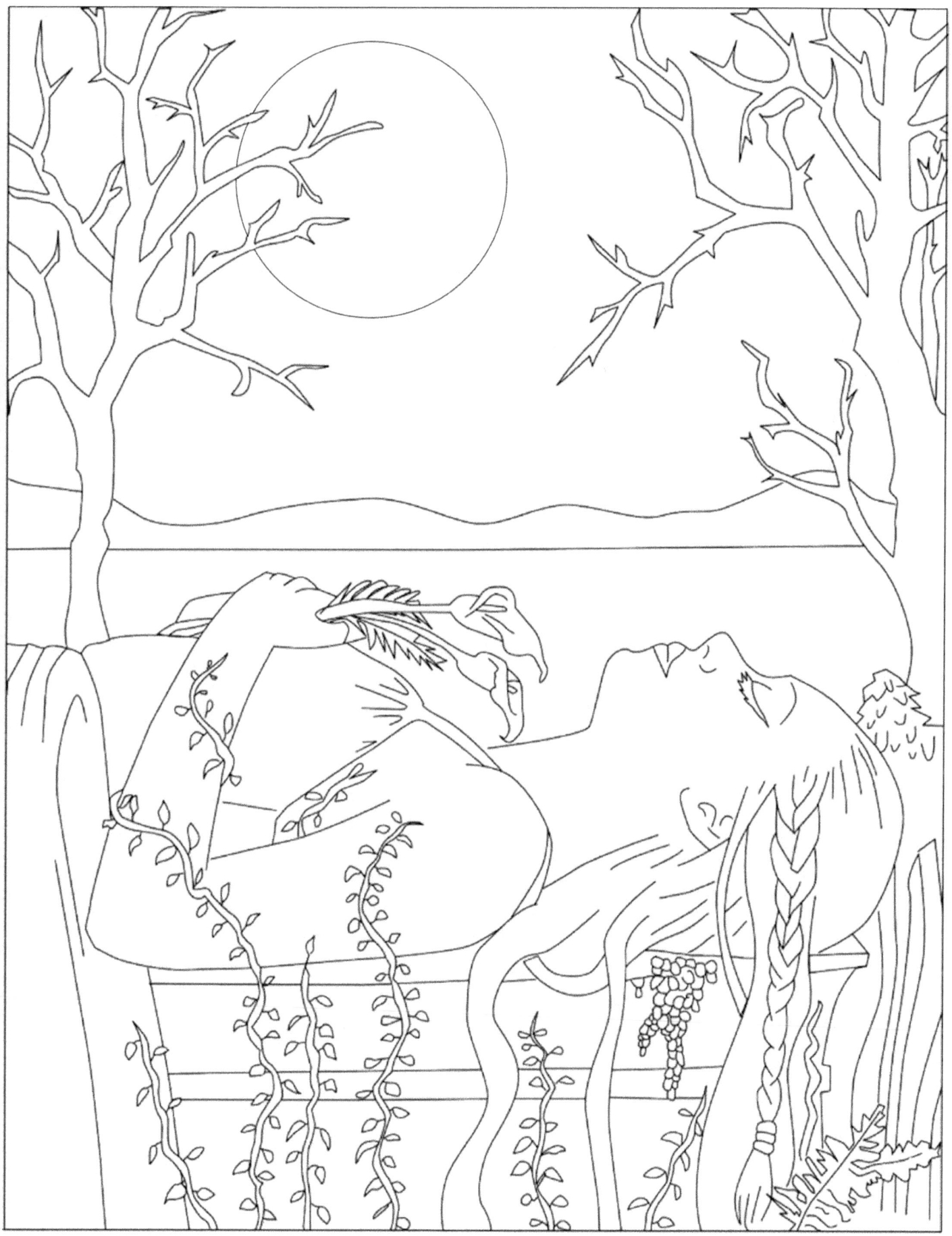

PRETTY & TWISTED

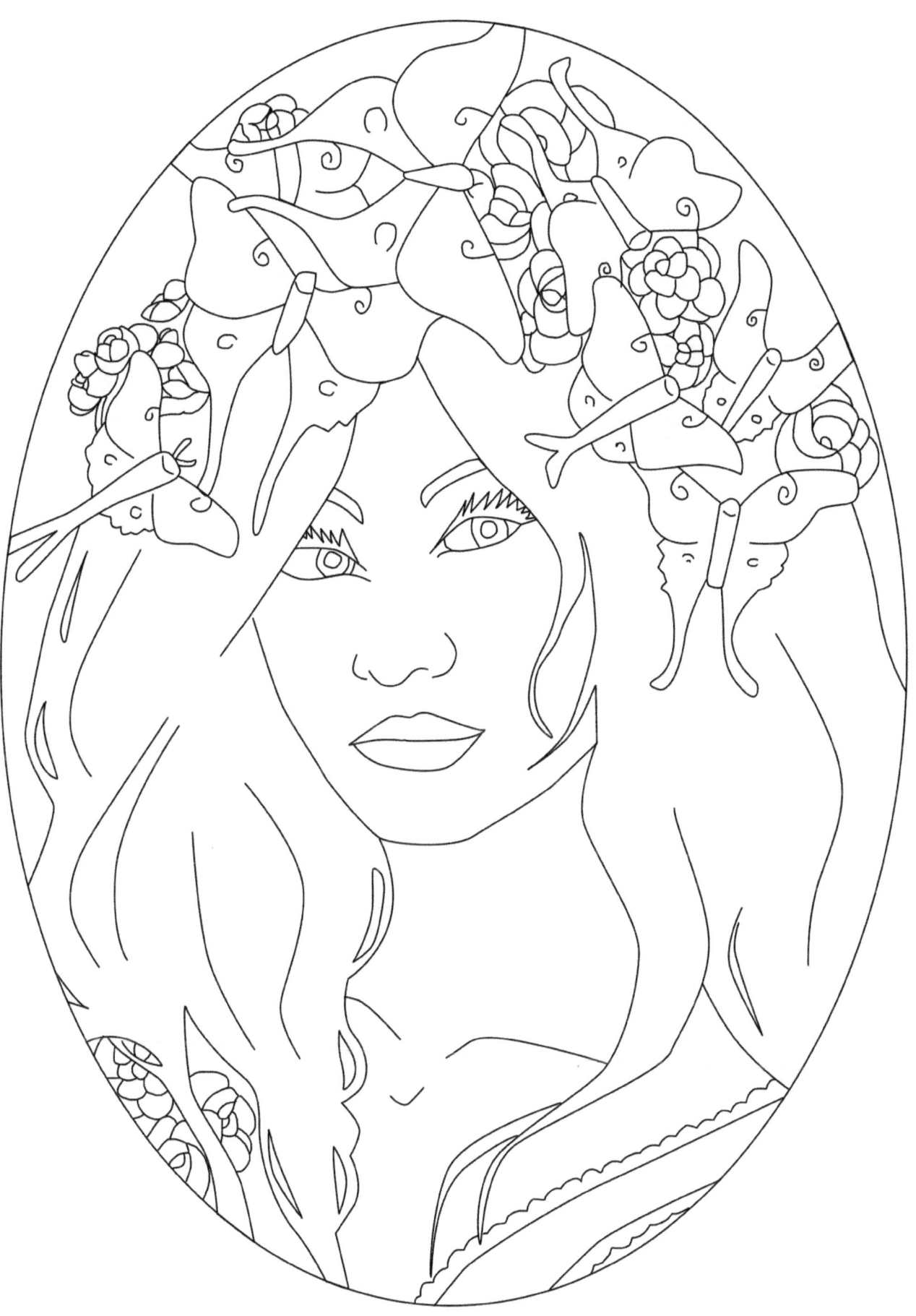

PRETTY & TWISTED

© Heather Rose

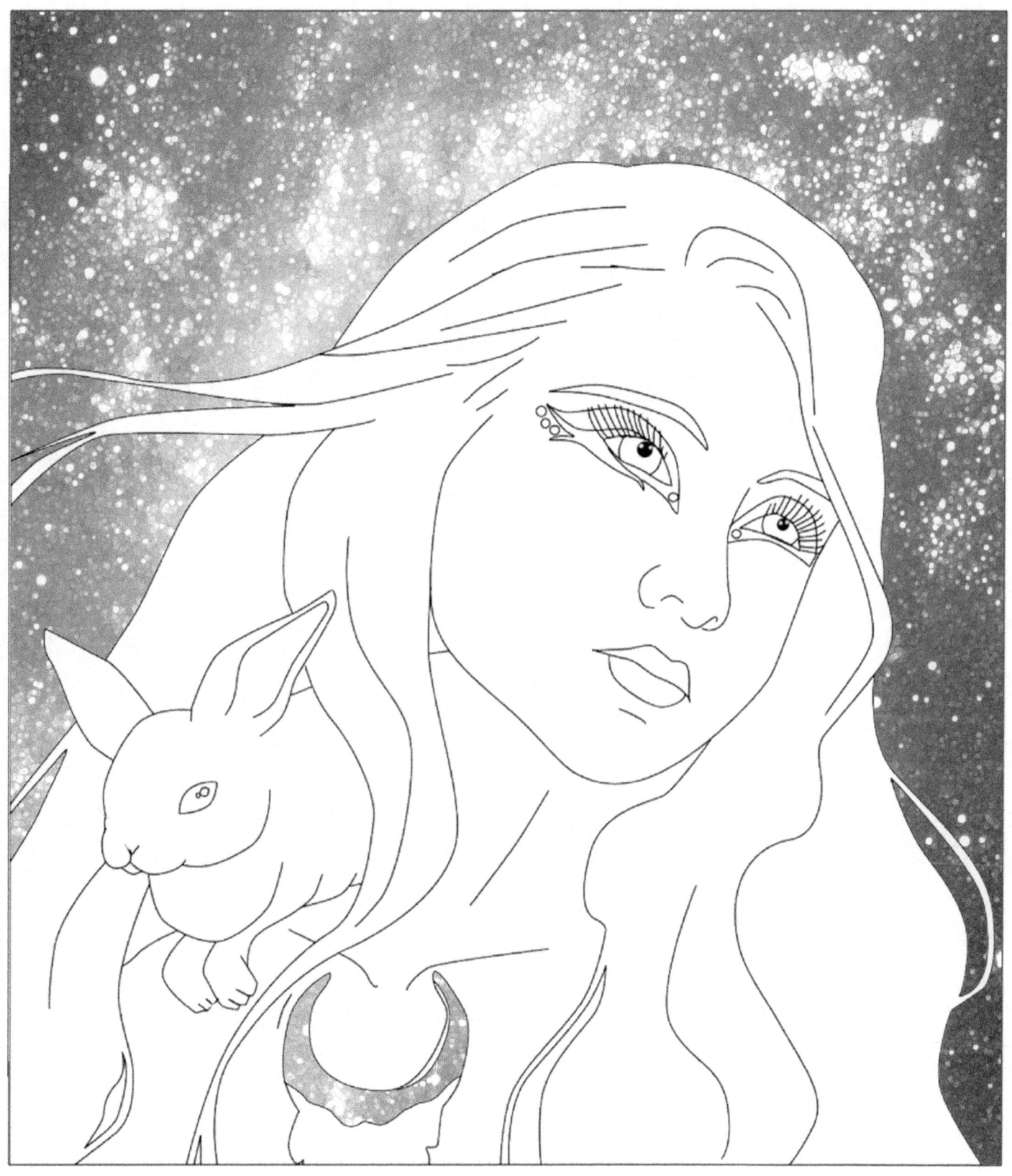

PRETTY & TWISTED

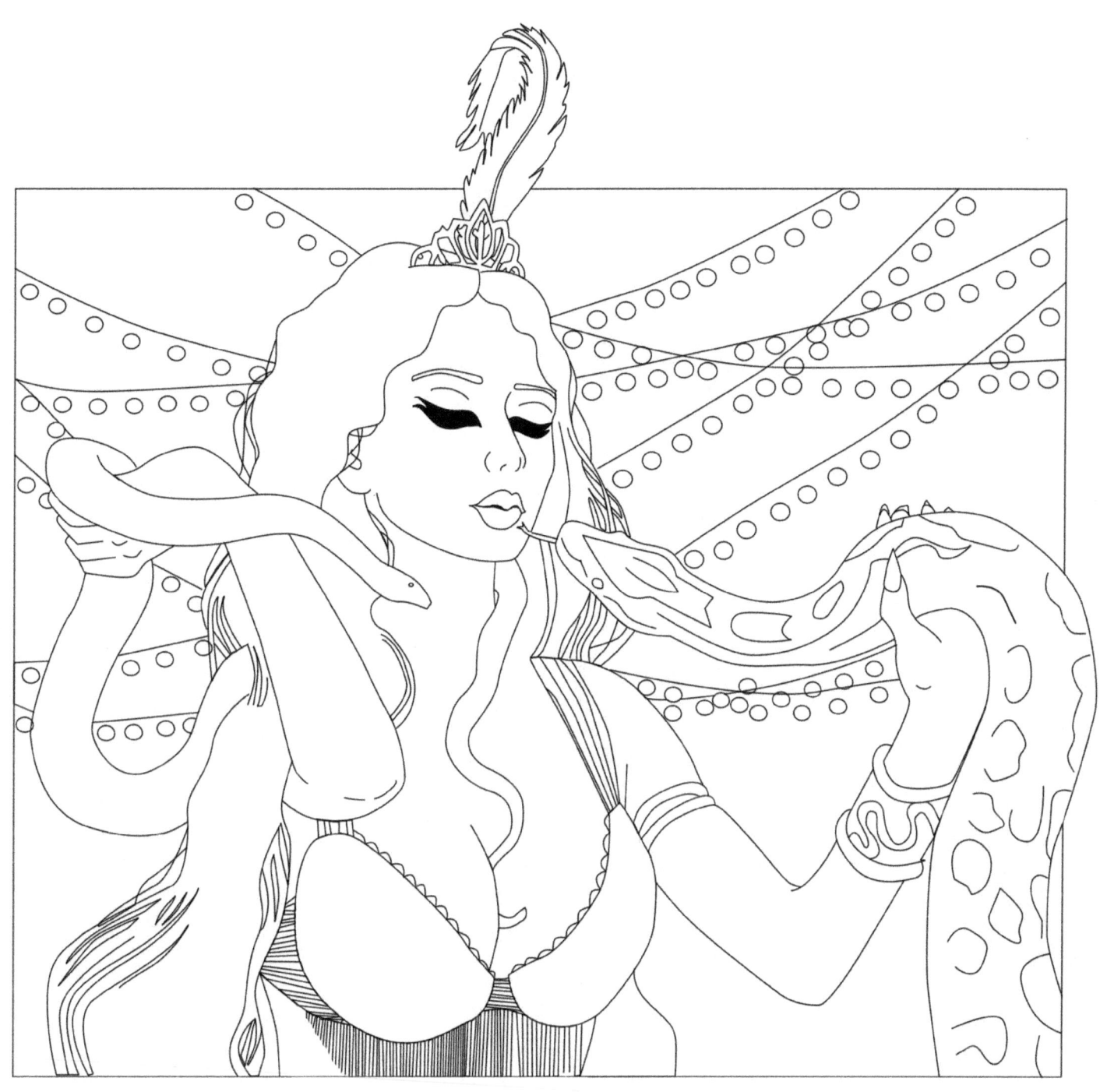

PRETTY & TWISTED

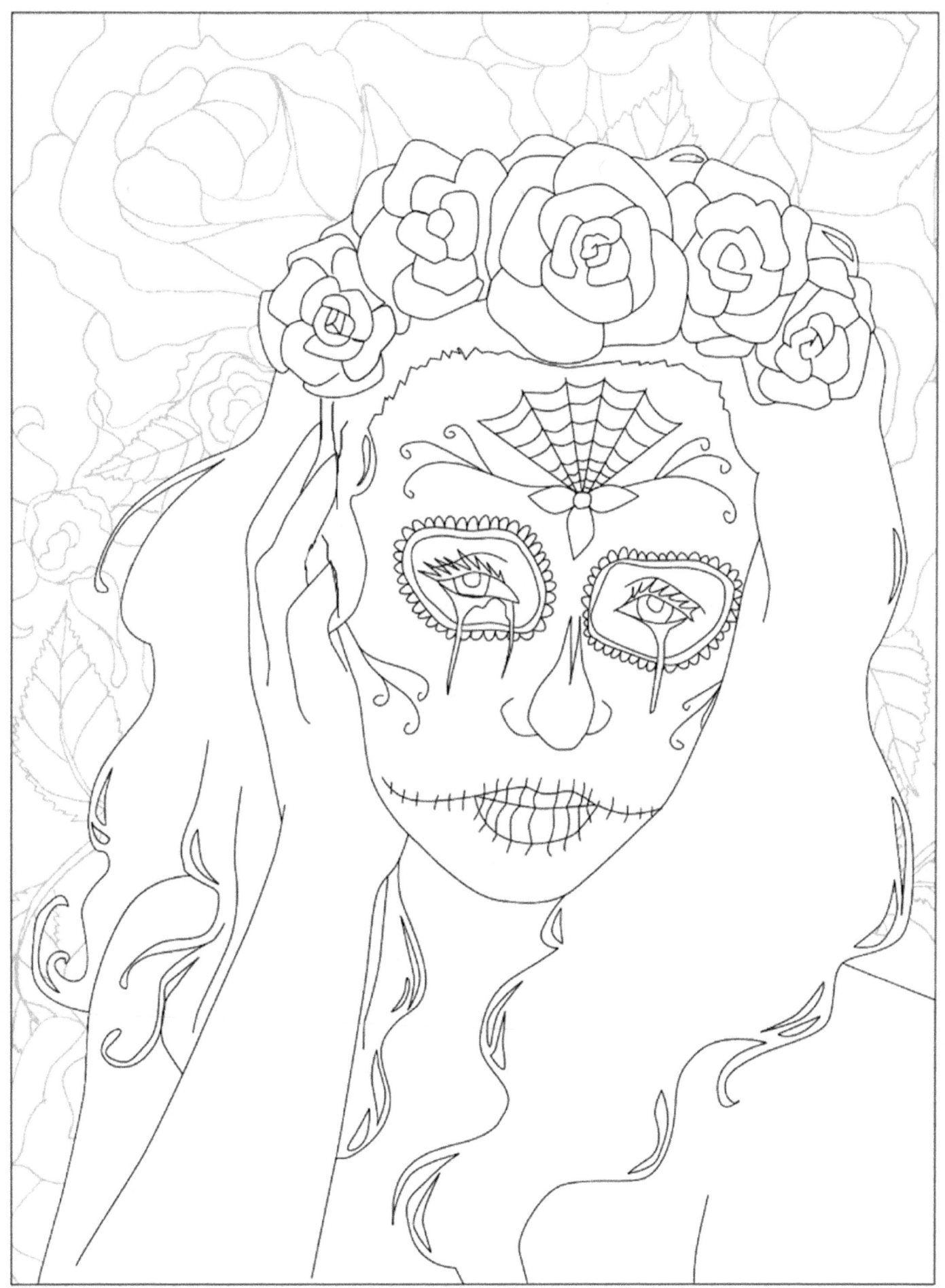

PRETTY & TWISTED

© Heather Rose

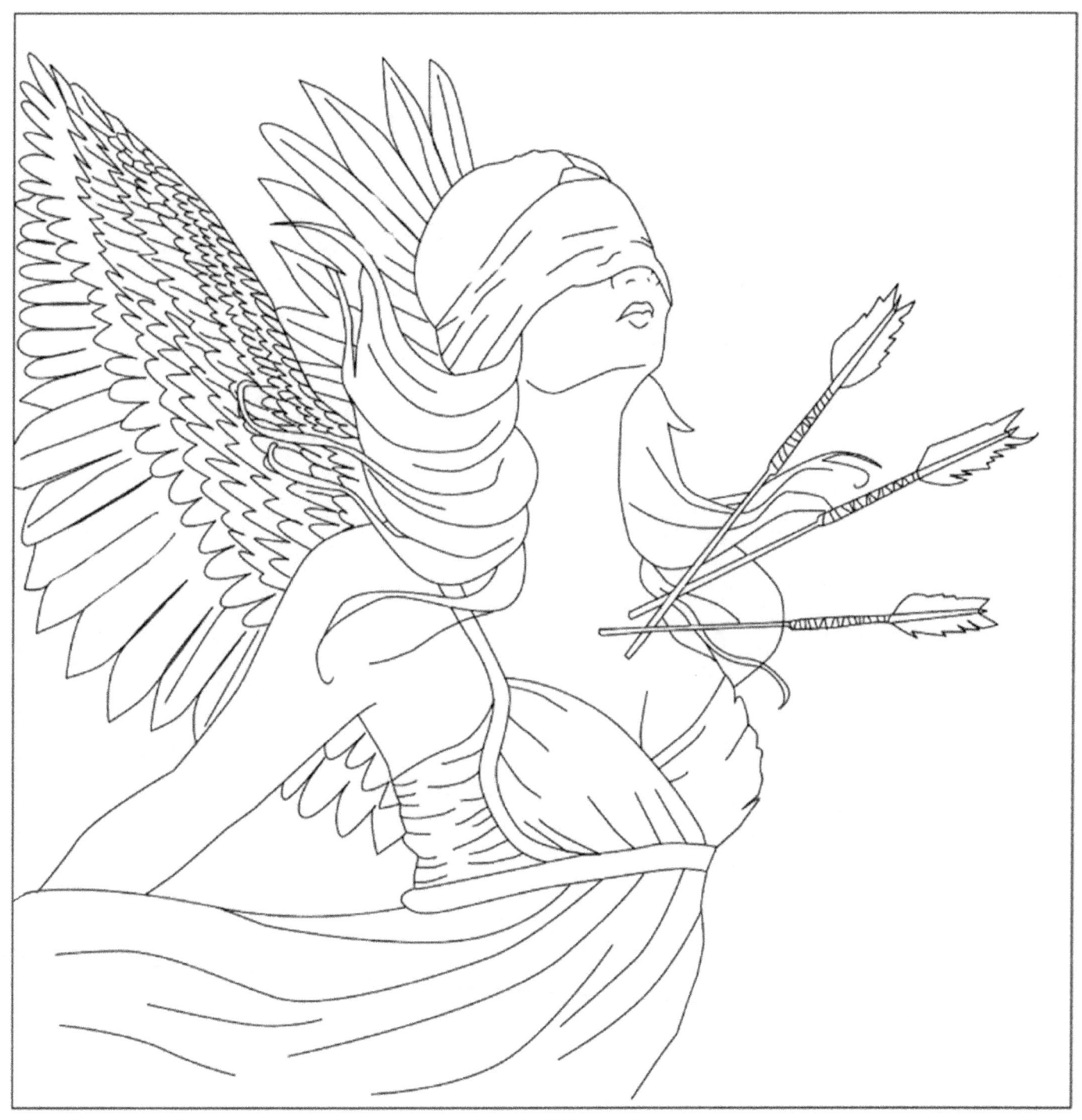

PRETTY & TWISTED

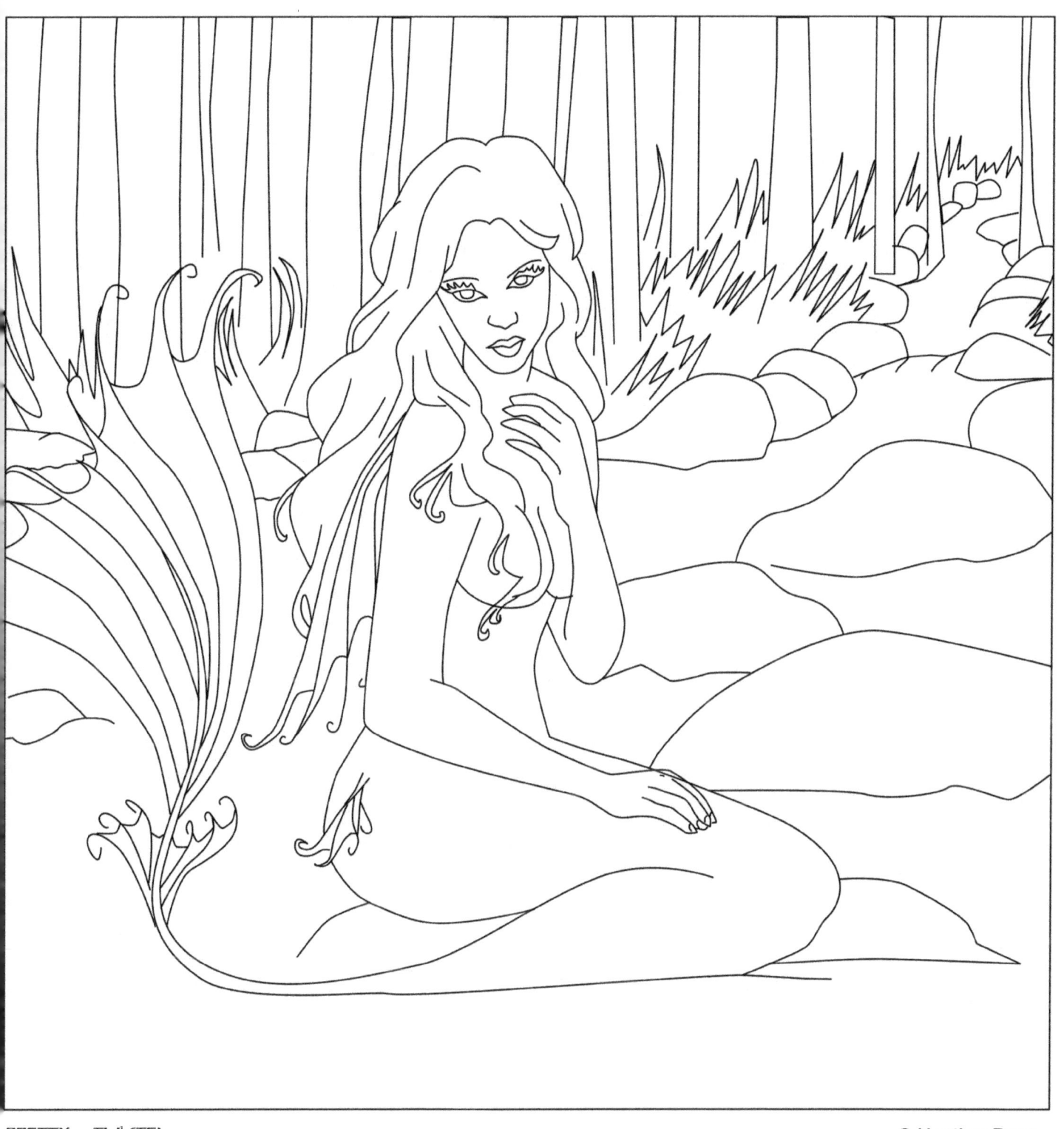

PRETTY & TWISTED

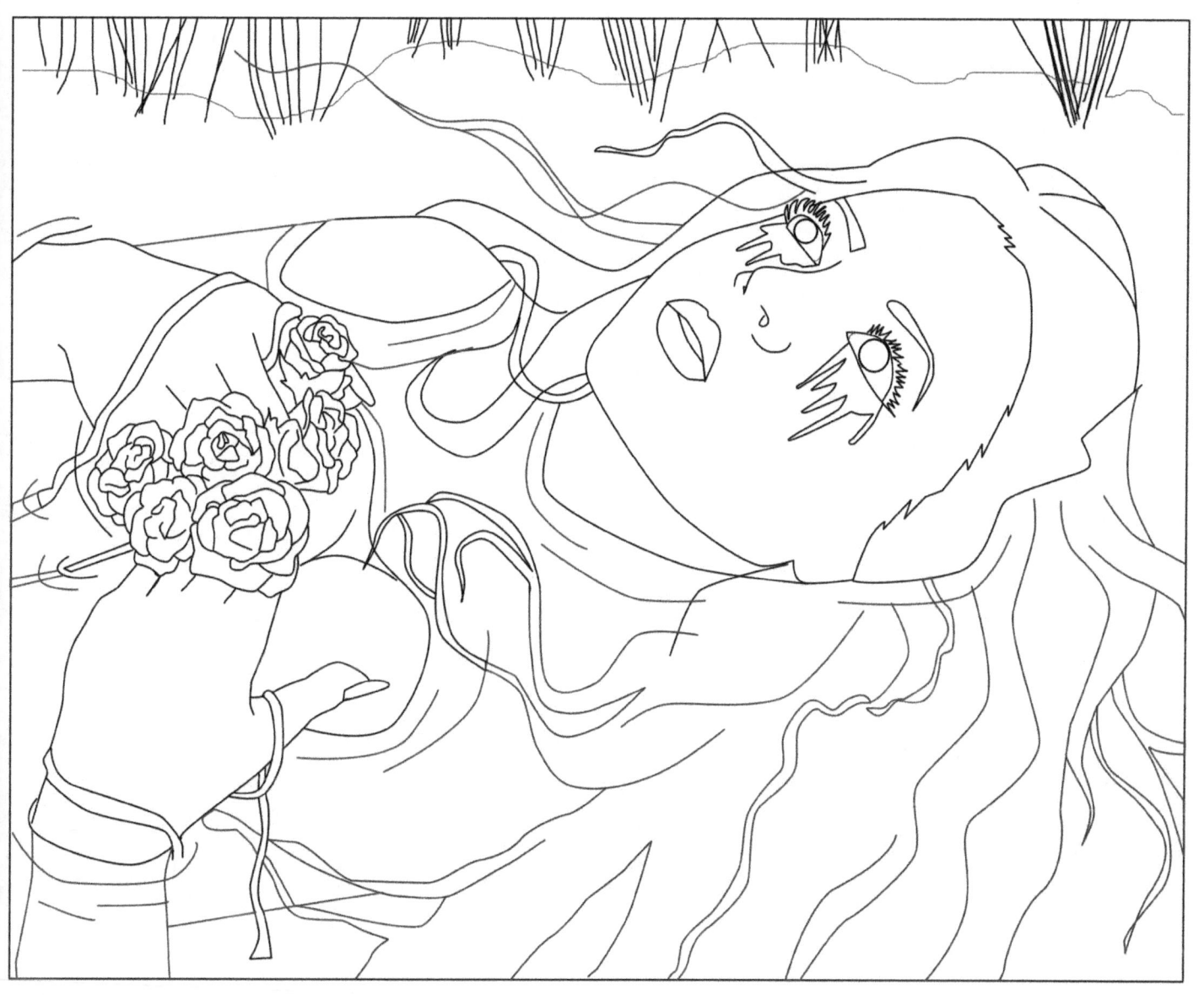

PRETTY & TWISTED

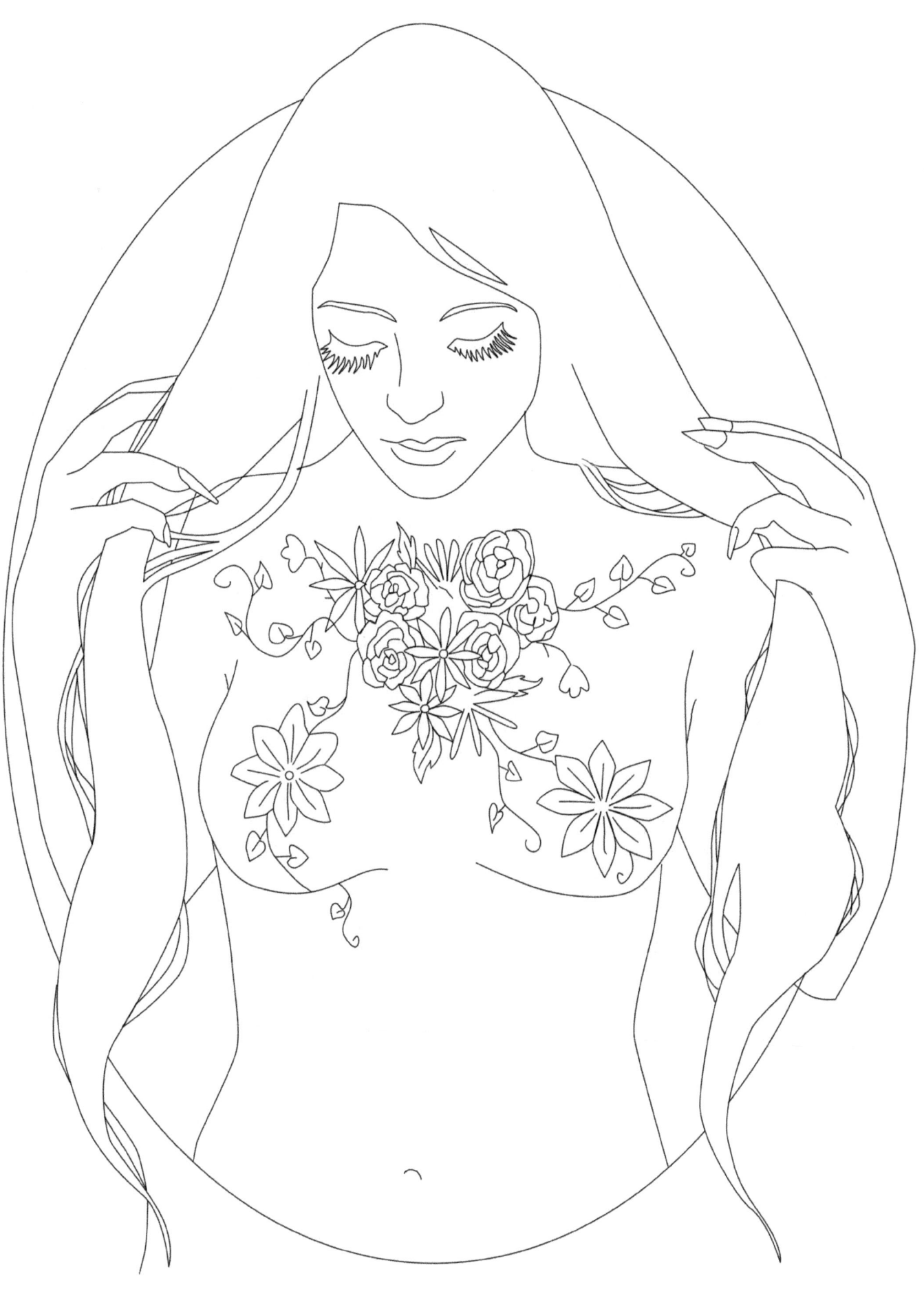

PRETTY & TWISTED

© Heather Rose

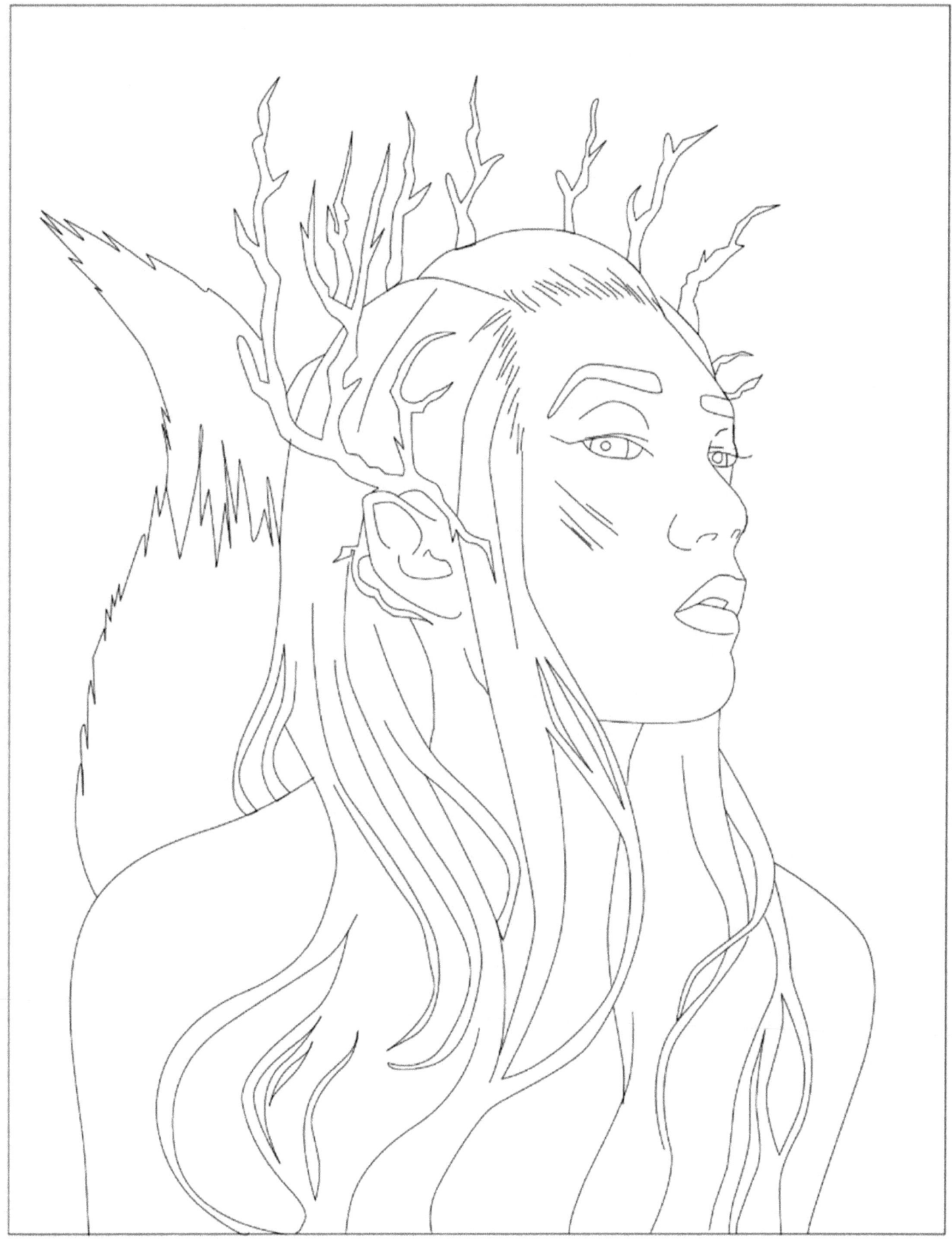

PRETTY & TWISTED

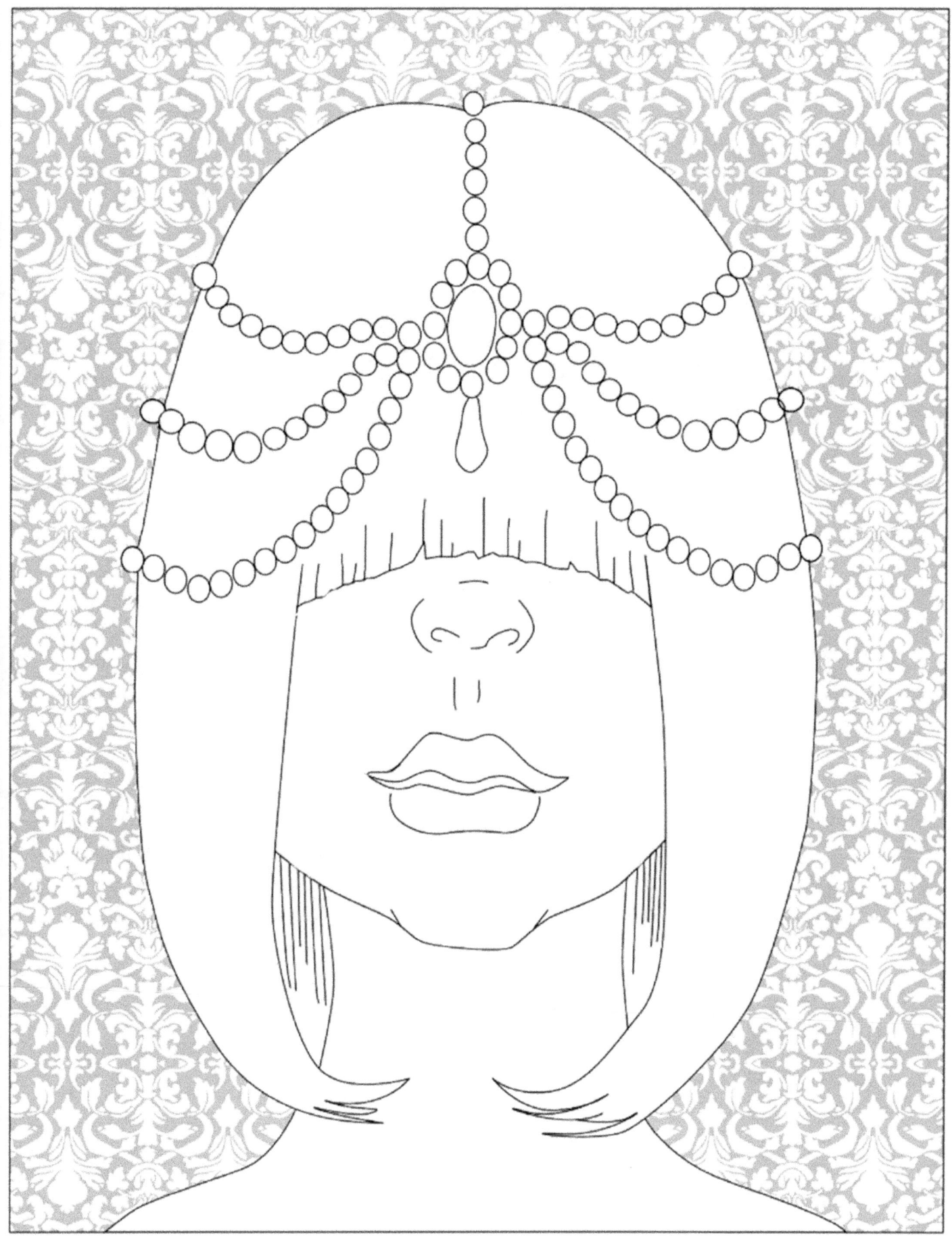

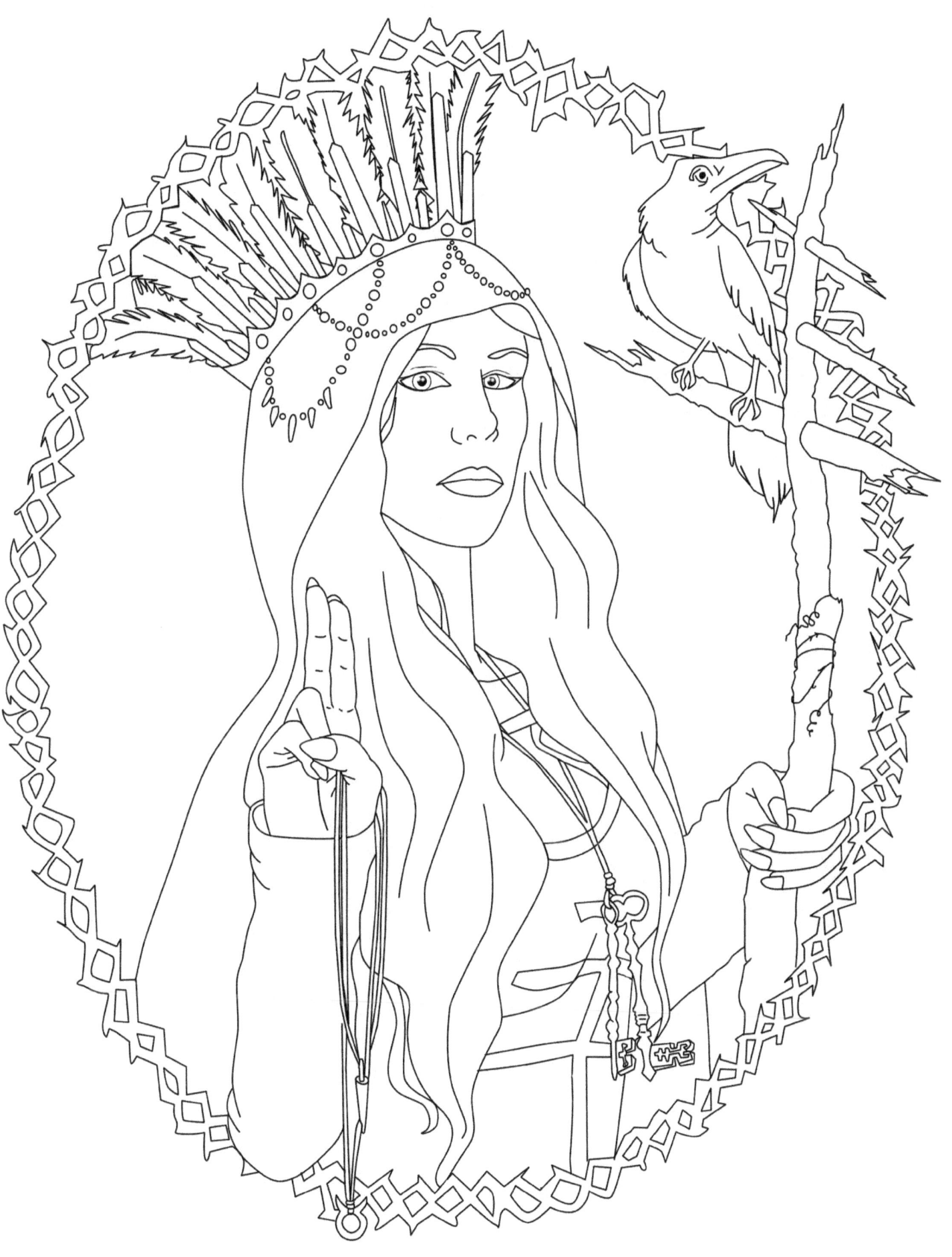

PRETTY & TWISTED

© Heather Rose

Heather Rose is a conceptual portrait artist from New England.
Specializing in dark and surreal figurative work, she creates bizarre worlds with
a touch of sensuality. She works mostly in pastels, acrylic, ink, and graphite, but
dabbles in everything from silkscreen printing to studio photography.

When not making art, she can usually be found
wandering through a forest or photographing hockey.

See all of Heather's work at Smoke-and-Honey.com

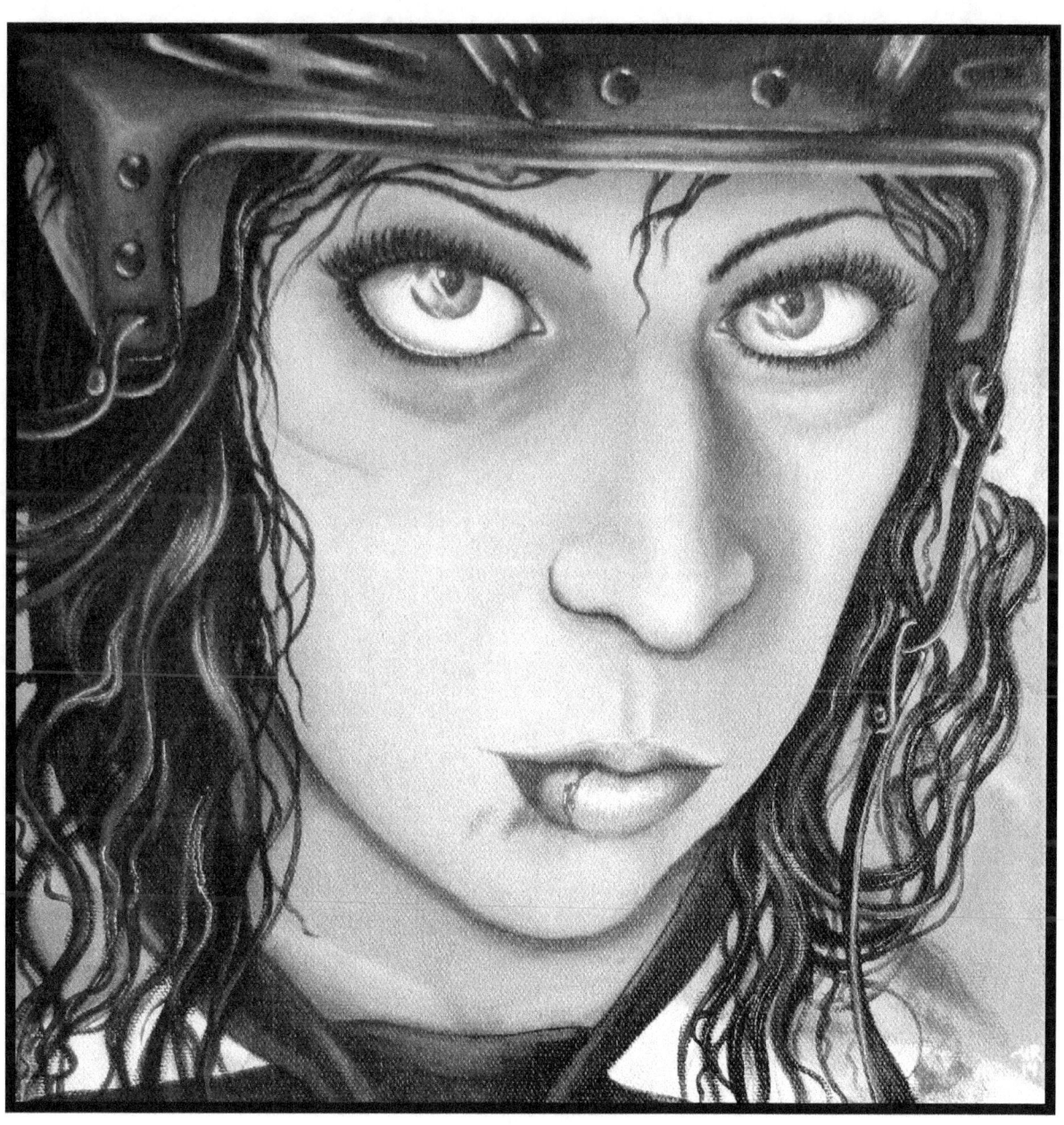

Thank you for supporting independent artists!